Maa Heeraben
and
Narendra

MAA HEERABEN AND NARENDRA

A Moving Story

ARVIND CHATURVEDI

BLOOMSBURY
NEW DELHI • LONDON • OXFORD • NEW YORK • SYDNEY

BLOOMSBURY INDIA
Bloomsbury Publishing India Pvt. Ltd
Second Floor, LSC Building No. 4, DDA Complex, Pocket C – 6 & 7,
Vasant Kunj, New Delhi, 110070

BLOOMSBURY, BLOOMSBURY INDIA and the Diana logo
are trademarks of Bloomsbury Publishing Plc

First published in India 2025

Copyright © Arvind Chaturvedi, 2025
All photographs courtesy of the Prime Minister's Office,
unless otherwise mentioned

Arvind Chaturvedi has asserted his right under the
Indian Copyright Act to be identified as the Author of this work

All rights reserved. No part of this publication may be: i) reproduced or transmitted
in any form, electronic or mechanical, including photocopying, recording or by
means of any information storage or retrieval system without prior permission in
writing from the publishers; or ii) used or reproduced in any way for the training,
development or operation of artificial intelligence (AI) technologies, including
generative AI technologies. The rights holders expressly reserve this publication
from the text and data mining exception as per Article 4(3) of the Digital Single
Market Directive (EU) 2019/790

ISBN: PB: 978-93-61319-75-4; eBook: 978-93-61319-76-1
2 4 6 8 10 9 7 5 3 1

Typeset in Fournier by Manipal Technologies Limited
Printed and bound in India by Replika Press Pvt. Ltd.

To find out more about our authors and books visit www.bloomsbury.com
and sign up for our newsletters

Contents

Preface   vii
Acknowledgements   xi

1. Maa Is Gone   1
2. Maa's Childhood and Challenges   15
3. Family Responsibility   21
4. Mother the Teacher, Narendra the Disciple   27
5. Child's Mischiefs, Mother's Teachings   35
6. From Birth to School: Mother's Influence on Narendra Modi   47
7. Deities, Faith and Belief   55
8. Father's Teachings   65
9. Heeraben's Concerns   69
10. Family Livelihood and Parental Imparting: A Boon for Politics   73
11. Prayers Answered   79
12. It Starts at Home   83
13. Blessings and Counsel   87

Contents

14.	Catalyst for Tomorrow	93
15.	Narendra's Asceticism, Mother's Support	97
16.	Maa's Sense of Service and Home Remedies	105
17.	Mother's Political Message	111
18.	When Narendra Modi Speaks of His Mother	117
19.	Guru's Service Was Rendered, But...	121
20.	Heeraben's Cuisine: A Taste of Love and Nostalgia	129
Notes		135
About the Author		139

Preface

In 2023 I met Prime Minister Narendra Modi when I went to present him with a copy of my book *Modi ka Banaras*. During the meeting that lasted fifteen to twenty minutes I found him to be an excellent listener who likes to learn from the people he interacts with. I told him about my two books on him. The first, *The Real Modi*, is an account of Narendra Modi's life related through anecdotes, stories and personal interviews with people close to him. *Modi ka Banaras* traces his journey from Gujarat to Varaṇasi and the impact he has had on Banaras since winning a Lok Sabha seat from that constituency.

In private, Modi speaks in measured tones. He is as eager a speaker as he is a listener. I had read Modi's books and knew that he had a difficult childhood but had exhibited leadership qualities from a very young age. That day he told me how he had collected funds for the construction of a

Preface

wall in B.N. High School when he was a student there. He learned early on not to be struck down by adversities but to overcome them and take people along. This helped him accomplish near-insurmountable tasks.

As I left the meeting, my mind was abuzz with questions about Modi. He came from a non-political family, but he had scaled such heights in politics. How did he achieve this feat? How did he become such a disciplined person?

I wondered if his mother, Heeraben, had had a hand in moulding Modi. A child learns everything from his mother. The mother is the most important part of an infant's life. She is the one he sees the most and she tends to his every need. She puts up with a lot of hardship to provide the best for her child and protect him from the world. Heeraben was indeed one such mother.

Narendra Modi and Heeraben shared an extraordinary relationship. I recalled Vivekananda's saying on being in charge of your own destiny: 'Bury the past which is dead and embrace the limitless possibilities of an unknown future.' I also recalled Darren Hardy's message

Preface

in *The Compound Effect* that small, everyday steps taken consistently and with conscious intent can help you achieve your dreams. Every word of yours, every thought and every action decide your destiny. At birth a person's life is a blank sheet. What he writes on it moulds his destiny. In Modi's case, Heeraben was the architect of his destiny. I realised she deserved a book on her life, and I decided to write it.

Acknowledgements

First of all, I would like to thank all those people who supported me in every difficult situation, showed me the way and encouraged me when I felt disappointed. I am very grateful to Prime Minister Narendra Modi for every mention of this mother in his writings and books; it is the inspiration of the mother, it is just a matter of understanding. I have read those books many times and have quoted many of these stories in this book.

During the writing of this book, I was in constant touch with Hiren Bhai Joshi, the prime minister's OSD (C&IT). His suggestions were very important to me. In spite of his packed schedule, he always answered my questions promptly. Thank you, Hiren Bhai, from my heart.

My wife, Preeti, currently lives in Lucknow for the education of our children, and I mostly live in Delhi. During the writing of this book, whenever

Acknowledgements

we talked on the phone, I would interrupt, saying, 'Now hang up, I am writing a book.' Then Preeti would say, 'Don't forget to write in it how many priceless moments I have lost while you wrote this book.' They say not everything is determined in life; some things are determined by your hard work and some by your destiny. Let's see where destiny takes us now. I am grateful for Preeti's support.

My elder daughter, Divyashree, who is currently studying in Delhi, has always encouraged me. Whenever I return from the office, she asks, 'Don't you have to write your book today?' Her constant curiosity has given me a lot of energy. My younger daughter, Aditi, gave many suggestions related to writing. I am grateful to my son, Atharv, who generously lent me his time while I wrote this book.

I have no words to thank my father. Today he is almost seventy-seven, yet he does not want to take any help from his sons. He prefers to work on his own in Varanasi. My brothers, who never asked me for anything but always gave their blessings, continue to inspire me. My sister-in-law ably looks after our house in Varanasi after our mother's departure, ensuring we don't feel the void.

Acknowledgements

Thanks to the simple and gentle Shashikant Tripathi ji and Shashikala Tripathi ji from the bottom of my heart. They always inquired about the progress I was making with the book, which was a source of inspiration for me. I also want to thank Chandravati Mishra ji. She too has been an inspiration while I was writing this book. I want to dedicate this book to my friend and brother-like figure, Mahendra Ranga ji, who was the principal chief commissioner of Central Goods and Service Tax (CGST), and Central Excise. Thank you to Sunil Bansal ji, national general secretary of the Bharatiya Janata Party. Whenever I am in trouble, he shows me the way. Thanks to Mahendra Ranga Sir.

Thanks also to those currently serving in the Indian government in Rajasthan, who never forget to inquire about my well-being every few days. Elder brother Manoj Singh, who is currently the chief secretary of the forest department in Uttar Pradesh, has always helped keep my spirits high. I am grateful to my elder brother and comrade Samir Tripathi, who stood by me in difficult situations, and to Vinay Srivastava, who supported and encouraged me on every occasion.

Acknowledgements

I express my heartfelt gratitude to Nitin Valecha of Bloomsbury, who consistently remained a source of encouragement for me, and to Pragya Banka, who edited this book.

Heartfelt thanks to Ved Prakash ji, working as OSD to the railway minister, whose latest ideas have always energised me.

In conclusion, I would say that on this earth, a mother is a magician for her children who wants to fulfil every wish of her son or daughter in an instant. A mother is a wonder, a mystery; you can never fully understand her. She lives every day, every moment, only for her son or daughter. That's why a mother is great. No one can ever repay a mother's debt. I salute my departed mother.

1

Maa Is Gone

'When doubts haunt me, when disappointments stare me in the face, and when I see not one ray of light on the horizon, I run to the Bhagavad Gita and find a verse to comfort me, and I immediately begin to smile in the midst of overwhelming sorrow.'

Mahatma Gandhi

Heeraben left this world at 3.30 a.m. on 30 December 2022. She was in her hundredth year. Narendra Modi had celebrated her ninety-ninth birthday with her in June. She used to live in Gandhinagar with her youngest son, Pankaj Modi, in a three-room flat. But at the time of her passing, Pankaj was with his family in Karnataka, where he had a minor accident.

Maa Heeraben and Narendra

Heeraben had been admitted to the hospital when her blood pressure shot up on 27 December. She had been administered a battery of tests, and the reports showed all her parameters were normal. There was no cause for concern and doctors said she only had age-related problems. The hospital had issued a bulletin barely thirty-six hours ago, on 28 December, saying she was stable and would soon be fine.

Thus, her passing came as a shock to Modi. He felt utterly bereft. It was his mother he turned to whenever he felt sad or dejected. He would visit her in Ahmedabad and find solace after spending some time with her. She could feel his every pain and her hand on his head could take away that pain. She was her son's biggest support, and now she was no more. The mother who taught him life's lessons, who had the courage to speak the truth, had left her son alone.

During the course of writing *The Real Modi*, I met Dr R.K. Shah, Modi's close friend, at his home in Ahmedabad. Dr Shah was a fount of information on the Modis. He told me about the time Modi heard Heeraben was unwell. Modi was staying at the State Sangh office in Ahmedabad then. As soon as they heard that Heeraben was unwell, Dr Shah and Modi went to his mother's

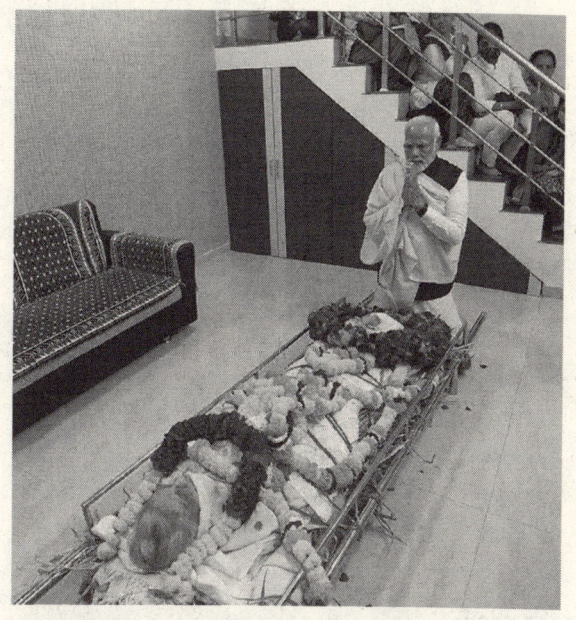

PM Narendra Modi paying his respects during his mother's last rites

house in Dr Shah's Fiat. Modi drove the car and they took her to the hospital. She was admitted there and soon recovered.

When I reached out to Dr Shah now, he said, 'It's so sad that Maa, who made him Narendra from ND, is no more.' Recalling Narendra Modi's visit to the United States in 2014, he said, 'I was sitting in Pankaj's small house in Ahmedabad listening to Heeraben narrate several stories from Narendra Modi's childhood. Her eyes were glued to the TV set to see her son and it was clear that her heart was with her son in America. She kept asking Pankaj to explain what was being said in English. She was a great soul. It seemed her life depended on her son. PM Modi also talked about all that he had learned from his mother in his public rallies or while addressing people

Maa Heeraben with author (from author's personal collection)

from a big stage. His mother always remained an inspiration for him. I have read biographies of many great people, but nobody eulogised their mother like Narendra Modi. This is why the entire nation wept when she passed away.'

When reports appeared in the media that Heeraben was in hospital, people across the nation had started praying for her health and quick recovery. They had never met her but had heard from her son stories of her struggles and sacrifices. They knew that she remained humble and did not move into the most famous address in the country. She had not availed herself of any facilities that came from being the prime minister's mother. In Prime Minister Narendra Modi's parliamentary constituency, Varanasi, people organised a 'Mahamrityunjaya' jaap, which is believed to grant immortality, protect against disasters and prevent premature death. Many observed fasts and offered special prayers, but in vain.

All that is left now are memories of her, her teachings and her thoughts. She was Shakti, a thread that kept everyone together. As the Gita says, '*Yat yat acharati shreshtha, tat tat ev itarah* [Whatever a great man does, so do others too; whatever way he behaves, others act accordingly].'

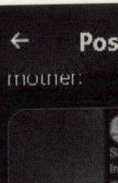

Prayers and messages on Heeraben's passing

President Biden ✓
@POTUS · Follow

Jill and I send our deepest and heartfelt condolences to Prime Minister @narendramodi on the loss of his mother, Heeraben Modi.

Our prayers are with the Prime Minister and his family at this difficult time.

4:15 AM · Dec 31, 2022

岸田文雄 ✓ · Dec 30, 2022
@kishida230 · Follow

PM Modi @narendramodi, I would like to express my deepest condolences for the passing of your beloved mother. May her soul rest in peace.

岸田文雄 ✓
@kishida230 · Follow

モディ首相 @narendramodiの御母堂の御逝去にお悔やみ申し上げます。心よりご冥福をお祈り申し上げます。

10:41 AM · Dec 30, 2022

♥ 3.7K Reply Share

Dr Philipp Ackermann ✓
@AmbAckermann · Follow

Deepest and sincere condolences to honorable Prime Minister @narendramodi. We join him and his family in mourning their loss.

10:47 AM · Dec 30, 2022

♥ 261 Reply Share

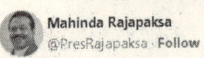

Mahinda Rajapaksa
@PresRajapaksa · Follow

Deeply saddened to hear of the demise of Smt. Heeraben Modi. My heartfelt condolences to Prime Minister @narendramodi ji on the loss of his beloved mother. Our thoughts and prayers are with the PM and his family in this hour of grief.

8:59 AM · Dec 30, 2022

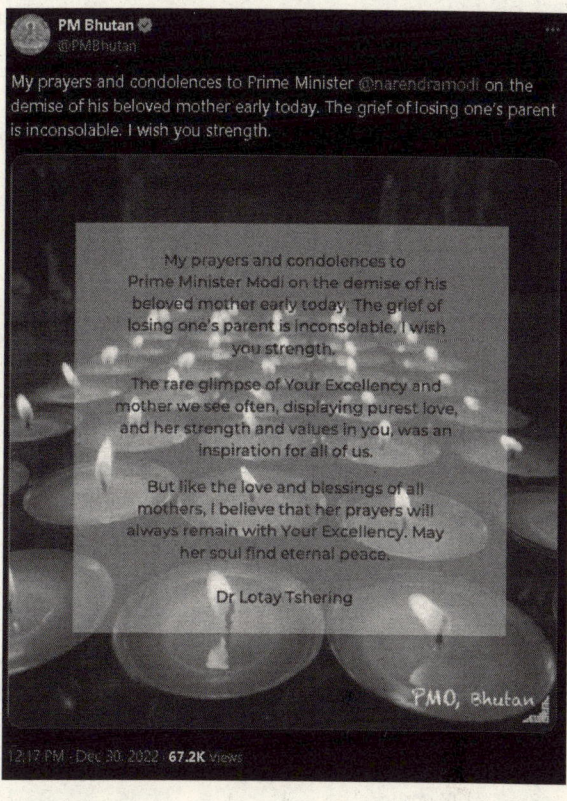

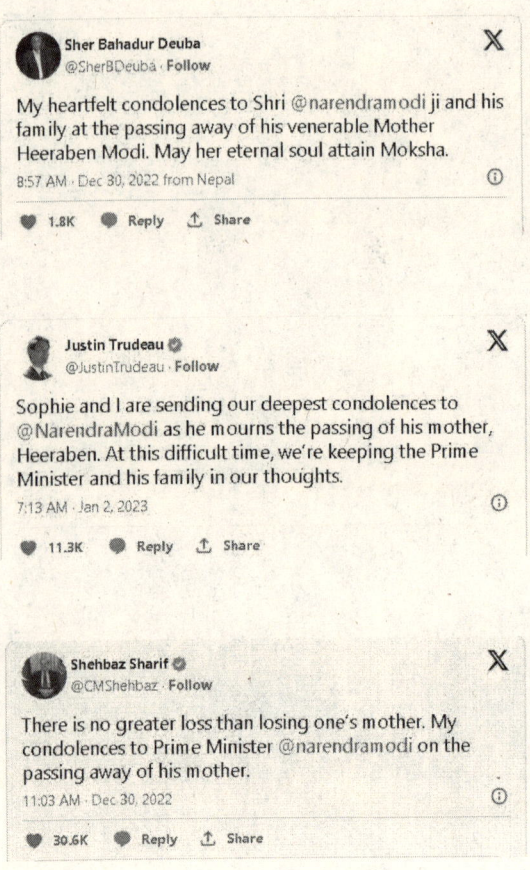

> **Sher Bahadur Deuba**
> @SherBDeuba · Follow
>
> My heartfelt condolences to Shri @narendramodi ji and his family at the passing away of his venerable Mother Heeraben Modi. May her eternal soul attain Moksha.
>
> 8:57 AM · Dec 30, 2022 from Nepal
>
> ♥ 1.8K   Reply   ⇧ Share

> **Justin Trudeau** ✓
> @JustinTrudeau · Follow
>
> Sophie and I are sending our deepest condolences to @NarendraModi as he mourns the passing of his mother, Heeraben. At this difficult time, we're keeping the Prime Minister and his family in our thoughts.
>
> 7:13 AM · Jan 2, 2023
>
> ♥ 11.3K   Reply   ⇧ Share

> **Shehbaz Sharif** ✓
> @CMShehbaz · Follow
>
> There is no greater loss than losing one's mother. My condolences to Prime Minister @narendramodi on the passing away of his mother.
>
> 11:03 AM · Dec 30, 2022
>
> ♥ 30.6K   Reply   ⇧ Share

Maa Is Gone

The prime minister was once asked why his mother did not stay with him.[1] Modi said that had he become prime minister when he was staying with his family at home, he would probably have wanted his mother and family beside him. But he had left home at a very young age and therefore never had any attachment to it. He had once brought his mother to Delhi, and they had stayed together for some time. But his mother always said he should not waste his time with her. Also, when she was with him, she had no work to do, whereas in the village she met a lot of people and interacted with them. And now, as prime minister, he too had no time for her as he was busy with official duties. 'I rarely got time to even have a meal with her. This used to pain me as I returned home at midnight and found her waiting for me,' he said.

Political leaders cutting across parties reached out to the prime minister to express their support for him and prayed for his mother's speedy recovery. Taking to X (then Twitter), Congress leader Rahul Gandhi said, 'The love between [a] mother and son is immortal and very precious. Modi Ji, I am with you in this difficult time. I hope that your mother recovers soon.' Congress president Mallikarjun Kharge said, 'We wish for the good health of Prime Minister Narendra Modi ji's mother. Hope she gets well soon.' Akhilesh Yadav, president of the Samajwadi Party, said, 'I wish a speedy recovery to Heeraben.' Mayawati, national president of the Bahujan Samaj Party, wished 'Heeraben a speedy recovery and good health'.

After the passing of his mother, everyone mourned with Narendra Modi. Leaders from around the world sent condolences to India's prime minister. Sri Lankan President Ranil Wickremesinghe tweeted that he was deeply saddened by the demise of Modi's mother and extended his heartfelt condolences to Modi and his family. Japanese Prime Minister Fumio Kishida wrote, 'I would like to express my deepest condolences on the passing of your beloved mother. May her soul rest in peace.' India's President Droupadi Murmu said, 'The entire life of PM Modi's mother Heeraben is a symbol of Indian ideals. My condolences to the family.' BJP national president J.P. Nadda wrote, 'The life of Heeraben is an inspiration.

The country received successful leadership due to her affection and honesty.'

Paying homage to his mother, Narendra Modi wrote, 'An amazing pause in the chariots of the century. Mother, I have always experienced that trinity in whose feet a yogi's journey, a symbol of a selfless karma yogi, and a dedicated life towards values remain contained.'[2]

Heeraben was supreme. Her life and her actions are a message of sacrifice, penance and dedication that will inspire the nation and the world. She changed her circumstances through her actions and gifted the nation a son who is changing its fortune.

2

Maa's Childhood and Challenges

'If the sun's rays are focused through a lens, they have the capacity to burn a hole. Similarly, if we concentrate our energies, we can use their power for the welfare of mankind.'

Mata Amritanandamayi

Heeraben was born on 18 June 1923. The day was significant in the life of the nation too as it was on that day that National Flag Day was celebrated in Nagpur.[1]

Heeraben's story is one of courage, hope, confidence and perseverance. It is the story of a normal, routine life. At the same time, it is the story of never giving up, of a pure heart and a dignified personality who was determined to achieve what she had set out to do. It is also the story of millions of girls in the country who face challenges in every sphere of life every day. The dedication and determination of some set them apart from others.

Heeraben's father, Hargovinddas Dajjidas Modi, ran a small hotel in Visnagar. It was customary in his household for a woman to deliver her first child at her parents' home. Thus Heeraben was born at her maternal grandparents' home in Palanpur, Gujarat. All customs were duly followed at Heeraben's birth. But within six months, her mother passed away. Prime Minister Narendra Modi has written in his blog that his mother lost her mother to an epidemic disease. Naturally, Heeraben had no memory of her mother's face or how it felt to be in her lap.

Her father remarried after some time to Sita Ba, who was from Patan in Gujarat. Sita Ba took over the care of Heeraben. Hargovinddas Modi and Sita Ba had three daughters and a son. Being the eldest child, Heeraben had to take care of her siblings, which she did like a mother, bathing and feeding them. She handled almost every household chore. Sadly, Sita Ba also died when her children were still young. Hargovinddas Modi married for the third time. His third wife, Samo Ba, gave birth to

Maa's Childhood and Challenges

Visnagar – where Heeraben spent her early days (photo by author)

two sons and two daughters. The responsibility for all eight siblings fell on Heeraben's shoulders though she was merely a child herself. Two of her siblings died early. Heeraben learned from her struggles every day. Childhood drudgery and problems toughened her. Heeraben was not sent to school due to financial constraints.

Heeraben was not given to complaining and she learned early in life that she must make the most of whatever she had. She faced all adversities and challenges with courage and conviction. As H.G. Wells said, 'What you don't have is not important. What you have and how you use it is important.'

Not much is known about Heeraben's marriage except that she was fifteen or sixteen years old when she was married off to Damodar Das Modi. After marriage, Heeraben moved from Visnagar to Vadnagar, a short distance away. Marriage did not mean her hardships were over, instead her ever-increasing responsibilities only made her stronger.

Damodar Das Modi came from a large family that struggled to make a living. The Modi family belonged to Navdotra village in Banaskantha district. In the late nineteenth century Damodar's grandfather Maganlal Ranchhordas moved to Vadnagar hoping to run a provision store there. His son Moolchand's eldest son, Damodar Das Modi, was born in 1915.

The Modis belonged to the Ghanchi caste. Their traditional occupation was oil extraction by pressing seeds using stone mills. As the eldest daughter-in-law of the family, Heeraben assisted

Maa's Childhood and Challenges

them in this arduous task, as her brothers-in-law were very young.

So this was how Heeraben spent the first two decades of her life. Whether in Visnagar or Vadnagar, Heeraben never had it easy. But she exemplifies the saying that fortitude and determination give us the power to overcome every disappointment. She showed how resilience and willpower are the stepping stones to success.

3

Family Responsibility

Like Heeraben's family, her husband's too was a joint family – Damodar Das had five younger brothers: Narsinh Das, Narottam Bhai, Janjivan Das, Kanti Lal and Jayanti Lal – but the command was with Heeraben. Her opinion was very important in every decision at home. She walked shoulder to shoulder with her husband, Damodar Das Modi, and engaged not only in household chores but also in employment activities.

Vadnagar was a small village lacking in basic facilities. Heeraben's day began when she woke up in the wee hours of the morning. Writing about his mother, Narendra Modi says, 'My mother was the eldest child in her family. After marriage too she was the eldest daughter-in-law. Even as a child she used to take care of every

Maa Heeraben and Narendra

Damodar Das Modi and Heeraben

Vadnagar – where Heeraben set up home with Damodar (photo by author)

small thing in her house. She always remained calm and composed even when she was under pressure and took care of her family.'

Family Responsibility

Mother's impact on Narendra Modi's childhood

During my visit to Vadnagar, I asked Narendra Modi's brothers and sister whom their mother loved the most. Prahlad Modi said their mother loved all the children equally. But Basanti said Narendra Bhai was their mother's favourite and that she loved him the most. She called him ND. She said that usually all children are dear to their mother, but Heeraben's love for Narendra Bhai was special. Whenever Heeraben fell ill while they were growing up, Narendra Bhai cooked food for everybody in the family.

Pankaj Modi also narrated an incident about the love between their mother and Narendra Bhai. He said the family normally ate millet roti with dal or some vegetable for lunch. But when guests came visiting, she served wheat roti with vegetables. On such days she would make an extra roti for Narendra Bhai, which she left on the tawa. The roti would become crisp, the way Narendra Bhai loved it. When he came home he would dip the roti in tea and relish it. Prahlad Bhai said that if any of the other siblings asked their mother for that special roti, she would refuse to give it to them.

Maa Heeraben and Narendra

Narendra Modi took time out of his hectic schedule to meet his mother. On his mother's birth centenary, Prime Minister Modi said in an article dedicated to his mother, 'The mother is the epitome of love, patience, trust and more. She not only gives us birth, she also shapes the child's personality and self-confidence. For her child she can neglect herself, forget herself.'[1]

Modi says that whatever good has happened in his life, it is because of his parents. He says his mother was very simple yet extraordinary, like any other mother. A mother's penance makes her child a good person, makes him sensitive. A mother is not a person but a symbol. As he was growing up, Narendra Modi watched his mother doing everything herself and learned from her. She never asked her children to help her. Narendra Modi has written that his mother never expected her children to neglect their studies and help her with her daily chores. A person never forgets what he has learned in childhood. His mother's struggles gave Narendra inspiration and strength.

Family Responsibility

Mahadev temple in Vadnagar (photo by author)

I spent several hours with Heeraben and Pankaj in Ahmedabad when I was writing my first book. Narendra Modi was then on a state visit to the United States. I wanted to hear from Heeraben how Modi was as a child. I will elaborate on the stories in the chapters that follow.

4

Mother the Teacher, Narendra the Disciple

After meeting Heeraben in Ahmedabad, I went to Vadnagar, which was second only to his mother in moulding Narendra Modi's personality.

Heeraben stayed in Vadnagar until her children grew up. This was her battleground. Vadnagar has a history that dates back 2,500 years. It is mentioned in the writings of the seventh-century Chinese traveller Xuanzang (Hiuen Tsang). Vadnagar also had Buddhist influences. One can still see Jain caves and monuments built by Solanki kings there.

Narendra Modi writes in the preface to his book *Jyoti Punj*, 'It is incredible that India has been able to keep its history alive.' About Kolkata's famous banyan tree, which is believed to be around 250 years old and spread over 1.89 hectares, Modi writes in the book:

> When I went there I was surprised to see the huge branches of the trees that were touching the earth. They were so huge that it was difficult to make out which one was the original tree. An employee present there told me that only senior officials who visit the place can answer my queries. The seed out of which the tree grew must have been lucky. First one tree grew out of the seed and gradually every branch became a tree in itself... Nobody built the tree. Some hungry bird ate a fruit and dropped its seed here. It could have dropped the seed anywhere in the world. Only a bird can perform such a mammoth task... If a man is determined to do something, he can do wonders. Like a small seed that grows into a huge banyan tree, man can achieve the impossible.

The metaphor seems apt for Modi today: he has become a banyan tree providing shade to Indians across the world.

Mother the Teacher, Narendra the Disciple

In Vadnagar I wanted to see the family house. There I met and spoke with several of Narendra Bhai's friends, relatives, neighbours, teachers and even his father's friends. They told me that most of them led difficult lives in those days as there were very few employment avenues in Vadnagar then.

Heeraben pitched in to supplement the family's income. She was an early riser and woke up at four every morning. Apart from working at home, looking after the extended family and extracting oil, Heeraben washed utensils and did other household chores in her neighbours' houses. She did not bother about the comments this inevitably attracted. She believed in the dignity of labour and was willing to go to any length to make her family comfortable. She also used to spin the charkha to earn money. She did not like to depend on anybody nor did she like to take anyone's help.

I would like to tell you a story that is apt for Heeraben. Once upon a time a king placed a huge boulder in the middle of a busy road and hid behind some trees to see how people would react to it. A lot of prominent people passed by and many of them criticised the king for the obstruction on the road. But no one bothered to remove the rock. Then came along a farmer carrying a sack filled with grains on his back. Placing the sack on one side, he started removing the rock. He found a bag filled with gold coins under the rock, along with a note saying that the gold coins were a gift for the person who removed the rock. The story teaches us that every hurdle we face in life brings an opportunity – if only we take the trouble to see it. If you can, you must try to make things right. This will bring you positive results. Every good deed comes back to you and your family. Similarly, Heeraben was rewarded for her readiness to help others.

Let's go back to the small lanes of Vadnagar. When I reached Heeraben and Damodar Das Modi's house, where all their children were born, I sat there for some time. It was now a double-storeyed building, but when the Modis lived there it had been a small single-storeyed house. We know from Narendra Modi's writings that the house had no windows, no toilets, no bathrooms. The roof was made of mud and bamboo frames. The family had to make do with a toilet that was covered by cloth on three sides. Prahlad Modi said that once the outer wall of the house had collapsed due to the rains. The house had no electricity and food was cooked on an earthen stove.

Narendra Modi saw his mother arranging for kerosene every evening. At times he too must have gone to buy kerosene. He must have seen his mother coughing because of the smoke emanating from the stove and felt her pain. Nilanjan Mukhopadhyay quotes Modi in his book *Narendra Modi: Ek Shaksiyat, Ek Daur* as saying, 'I led a miserable life because there was no electricity in the village where I grew up. We had to face a lot of difficulty in childhood.' So when he became the chief minister of Gujarat, he launched the Jyotigram Yojana.

In a speech delivered at Kamrej, Gujarat, on 30 September 2006, Modi recounted that when the Jyotigram Yojana was launched, Amarsinh Chaudhary, leader of the Opposition in the Gujarat Assembly, called on him. Chaudhary said, 'Narendra Bhai, you have just become the chief minister and have no experience. Somebody has misguided you. It is not possible to supply twenty-four-hour electricity in villages. As a friend I want to tell you that you are making a mistake. This scheme will fail.' Narendra Bhai jokingly replied, 'Amarsinh Bhai, if the task was so simple, people would have made you the chief minister. Because it is difficult, they have made me the chief minister.'[1] Kishor Makwana writes in his book *Modi: Common Man's PM* that when Modi took over as the chief minister of Gujarat for the second time in 2002, 18,000 villages in Gujarat started receiving twenty-four-hour, three-phase electricity under the Jyotigram Yojana.

Memories of the pain his mother, family and the villagers suffered were uppermost in his mind as he tried to help the poor in his capacity as chief minister. Addressing a public rally as the chief minister of Gujarat, Modi said, 'The country is going to celebrate sixty years of Independence. In 2010 Gujarat will also celebrate its fiftieth anniversary. However, even today women have to go for defecation in the open. They have to wait till it becomes dark and stay miserable till then. Even in modern times they have to face so much mental agony for defecation. It is a matter of disgrace for us.' He also gave the slogan '*Pehle sauchalaya, phir devalaya*' (First toilets, then temples).

The International Energy Agency and the African Development Bank published a report on access to clean cooking facilities in 2023. The report, *Vision for Clean Cooking Access for All*, states that 230 crore people in India cook food on traditional stoves in the open, using polluting fuels like kerosene, coal, wood and dung cake. The report also notes that India, China and Indonesia have made commendable strides in disseminating clean cooking technologies. Two years after becoming prime minister, Narendra Modi launched the Ujjwala Yojana in May 2016. Under the scheme around 9.6 crore gas connections have been provided so far to the needy. According to a World Health Organization report, air pollution kills around 32 lakh people every year. This includes 2.37 lakh children under the age of five.

Recalling their days in the Vadnagar house, Prahlad told me a story about their mother. 'It was late at night and our father wasn't home. Our mother was sleeping with our sister. She heard some sounds and woke up, wondering if someone had broken in. The brave daughter of a brave father, she confronted the thieves and chased them away. My paternal grandfather's family, on the other hand, was very simple and meek.'

But poverty forced the Modi family out of even this modest house. They sold the house, and the children moved out to different places for work. In his mother's birth centenary year, Narendra Modi said his mother had only seen poverty, which he described as something God had given – it was God's will. Modi writes that poverty and tension coexist. 'However, my parents were special. They never allowed any tension in the house.'

In Vadnagar Heeraben taught her children the value of honesty and purity, which can inspire collective good. These are lifelong qualities. Narendra Modi says in his book *Samuhik Hit Ka Deep Jale*, 'Do not worry about defeating anyone. You try to make progress from wherever you are. Test your limits every day so that you do not bow down in the face of adversity.'

It was because of his mother's teachings that Narendra Modi embarked on the difficult path fearlessly.

5

Child's Mischiefs, Mother's Teachings

Every parent has dreams of seeing their children progress. Heeraben and Damodar Das Modi were no exception. Despite their daily struggles, they kept the family together. I see Heeraben as a person who never felt intimidated by any crisis and never gave up. Everybody loves to dream but we have to work to achieve those dreams. And that cannot be done in a few days or months. Anything can be achieved with great effort. There is a saying about the African jungle: a deer may be slow, but it must run faster than the fastest lion to survive.

I see Narendra Modi as similar to the American adventurer John Goddard, who was barely fourteen when he put down his dreams in his diary: climb Mount Everest, swim across the

Nile River, etc. When Goddard turned sixty, he opened his diary and started ticking off his list to see how many goals he had achieved. He was surprised to see that he had accomplished fifty-five out of the fifty-seven goals he had listed.

We all have dreams but find it difficult to put in the hard work needed over a long period of time to fulfil them. Since childhood Narendra Modi had a habit of setting himself a target and then working towards it. He accepted challenges and did everything needed to achieve his goals.

I met Heeraben in Pankaj Modi's three-room flat in Gandhinagar. She kept it spick and span. The room was sparse. On one wall was a big picture of a guruji clad in saffron. A family photo stood framed on a table. She gave me a glass of water. As Pankaj was talking about their childhood, she kept smiling and nodding.

Mother's first lesson

The people of the country are familiar with the story of Sharmishtha Lake, having heard it from Prime Minister Modi. In Vadnagar almost everyone told me the story in their own words. They described Narendra Modi as someone

Child's Mischiefs, Mother's Teachings

extraordinary. Whoever I met in Vadnagar, be it Narendra Modi's family members, his teachers or his childhood friends, everyone said that he was special. Even as a child Narendra Modi knew how to take everyone along.

The Sharmishtha pond in Vadnagar is very big. Now there are pucca ghats around the pond. But when Narendra Modi went to swim there as a child, it had only bushes and trees around it. Narendra Modi would swim with his friends, winning and losing friendly races. Here I would like to give the example of Sachin Tendulkar, who once revealed the secret of his success to a journalist. He said he not only played cricket but lived cricket. He thought of the game in every waking moment of his life. In the two decades of his cricketing career, there was not a single day when he did not reach the nets for practice. Narendra Modi is somewhat like that. He is not satisfied with his victories and moves on to a new challenge the very next moment. Whether it was the playground of his childhood or the various tasks he performed after becoming prime minister, Narendra Modi always rehearses his next move.

Maa Heeraben and Narendra

Pankaj said that Narendra Bhai used to bathe for hours in the Sharmishtha pond with a group of friends. His mother washed their clothes mostly by the pond. Once a crocodile had laid eggs near the pond, and seeing so many hatchlings together, Narendra thought they would make good playthings. His friends also encouraged him. They decided to take the hatchlings home. Narendra picked one up and brought it home. Needless to say, Heeraben was shocked. After a moment's pause, she told him, 'Imagine if somebody picked you up and took you away, what would happen to me, your mother? I would not be able to live without you. Similarly, the mother crocodile must be crying and looking for her missing baby.' It was raining heavily in Vadnagar that day. Sharmishtha Lake was overflowing. But after hearing his mother, Narendra Bhai did not waste a moment and went back to return the crocodile baby to the lake.

Narendra Modi writes in his blog that a mother's prayers make her child a better human being. Motherly love makes her child sensitive. A mother is not just a person but a personality. She is the embodiment of godly virtues and manifests herself according to the level of one's perception.

Child's Mischiefs, Mother's Teachings

Mother's teachings

Drudgery in her childhood must have made Heeraben understand the value of everything. Everyday struggles in life teach you new things. Narendra Modi often speaks about his mother's efforts to conserve water. As a child he saw his mother collect rainwater and use it judiciously and he learned the importance of water conservation. Heeraben must have learned how to save water from her elders in the family. Hardly sixty kilometres from Vadnagar is the famous Rani ki Vav (Queen's Stepwell). Built somewhere between the tenth and twelfth centuries in limestone in the Maru-Gurjar style, it is sixty-four metres long and twenty-seven metres deep and must have served for centuries as an inspiration for water conservation to people living in the region.

Modi writes in his blog: 'Our house had become so dilapidated that its roof leaked when it rained. Mother would place utensils on the floor under the leaking roof to avoid flooding in the house. The rainwater used to collect in those utensils but I never saw Mother getting hassled or cursing herself. You will be surprised to know that Mother used that rainwater for the next two to three days in the house. What can be a better way of water conservation?'

As a child Narendra Modi saw his mother making several rounds every day to the well to fetch water. As a Rashtriya Swayamsevak Sangh (RSS) worker, he tried his best not to waste even a single drop of water. After leading the BJP to victory in the municipal elections in Ahmedabad as the party's general secretary, he gave many suggestions to the municipality to save water. Saving ponds in cities was one such suggestion. After becoming the chief minister of Gujarat, Narendra Modi launched many schemes in rural areas for water conservation. On becoming prime minister, he spread the message of water conservation throughout the country.

Modi says in his book *Samuhik Hit Ka Deep Jale*, 'Water is God's gift, his prasad. We should do penance and feel sorry if even a drop of water is wasted.' Water storage, water conservation and the correct way of irrigation are equally important. In 2016, Modi announced the government's decision to build five lakh ponds as agricultural reservoirs. He emphasised that every village should try to save water.

Child's Mischiefs, Mother's Teachings

Other initiatives launched by Narendra Modi to save water include Jalyukt Shivar, a scheme to transform water management in drought-hit Maharashtra; Lok Suraj, Jal Suraj Abhiyan in Chhattisgarh; and Kapildhara Koop Yojana and Balram Talab Yojana in Madhya Pradesh, under which 22,000 ponds have been built. Uttar Pradesh has launched Jal Bachao Abhiyan, while efforts are ongoing in Karnataka to save wells under Kalyani Yojana.

There are a number of bavadis (ponds), deep tanks and stepwells in Rajasthan and Gujarat. The prime minister often talks about the water management mission. In *Mann ki Baat* he once mentioned the Nag River, where 20,000 women came forward to revive the dying river. Modi also talked about Porbandar, the birthplace of Mahatma Gandhi, where there is a 200-year-old water spring just behind Bapu's house which even today helps conserve water. In another *Mann ki Baat*, the prime minister said that Gujarat and Andhra Pradesh are making use of technology for water conservation.

Mother was the biggest inspiration. The son could always feel the suffering that his mother endured while fetching water from afar in the immense heat of summer. This is why efforts are being made to supply tap water to every house across the country. Now no Heeraben will have to walk barefoot to fetch water from afar. The prime minister has said, 'Water is the basis of every life in this world and water is also the biggest resource. Even our ancestors stressed the need for water conservation. Our Vedas and Puranas all talk about the importance of saving water.'

Mother said nature is a gift; use it wisely

In an article dedicated to his mother, Modi writes, 'I found my mother using the gift of nature in the best way. Mother loved to keep her house always neat and tidy. She would work the whole day to decorate and make it look beautiful. She would wipe the floor clean with cow dung.' Modi further writes, 'You must have noticed that dung cakes cause smoke on burning. Mother would use dung cakes to cook food in the house which had no windows. The walls in the house would turn black with smoke. Every few weeks Mother would repaint the house walls which would make them look new.' Modi adds, 'Mother used to

Child's Mischiefs, Mother's Teachings

make beautiful bowls with mud and decorate the house with those bowls. Mother was a champion in recycling old stuff, a habit common among Indians.'

In his article, Modi also refers to his mother making papier-mâché. She used to soak pieces of old paper and grind them with tamarind seeds to make a glue-like paste. She used this to stick small pieces of glass on the walls to decorate the house, a common practice in Gujarat even now.

He writes that his mother was very conscious about cleanliness. 'Whenever I visited Gandhinagar, she would feed me sweets with her own hands. After feeding me, she would clean my face like a baby's.' He added that his mother always kept a towel or a handkerchief handy. He also said that she respected those engaged in sanitation work. He remembers the time a worker came to clean the drain near their house in Vadnagar. 'Mother would not let him go without having tea first. After some time even the sanitation workers knew if they wanted to have tea after work they could always come to our house.'

Narendra Modi writes in his blog, 'My mother would invite home every saint who was visiting anywhere near the house and feed them. When they were leaving, Mother would seek their blessings, not for herself but for us siblings. She would say, kindly bless my children so that they remain happy with others and also feel their pain. Bless them [so they may] instil the trait of selfless service and devotion in them.'

Father's command for Narendra

In the blog dedicated to his mother, Narendra Modi writes that he owes everything he has achieved in life so far to his parents. He writes about his father in the blog, 'Like clockwork, my father used to leave for work at four in the morning. His footsteps would tell the neighbours that it was 4 a.m. and Damodar Kaka was leaving for work. Another daily ritual was to pray at the local temple before opening his little tea shop.'

It's not easy to comprehend the truth. One must go deep to understand it. For example, when a person jumps from the springboard of a swimming pool for a deep dive, he has to hold his breath and come out with a smile. But when he emerges, he finds the world brighter than before. God may guide you to the path of truth, but

Child's Mischiefs, Mother's Teachings

you are the one who has to walk on it. Similarly, Damodar Das Modi also showed Narendra the right path as he knew that what you learn as a child helps you in life.

Pankaj shared a story about their father. Knowing that Narendra used to frolic in the Sharmishtha pond for hours with his friends with no fixed time to return home, their father gave him the task of taking care of their cow. Narendra Bhai had to bathe the cow and bring it home and he did this job diligently. This also made him a gau sevak from childhood.

His parents' teachings and their struggles taught Narendra Modi to serve others selflessly and to do something special for society.

6

From Birth to School: Mother's Influence on Narendra Modi

Narendra Modi is the third child of Heeraben, and they shared a deep connection since his birth. As Narendra grew older, their relationship deepened, and their conversations reflected their unique connection. When Narendra reached the age to begin school, his father arranged to send him and his cousin Narsidhas Mulchand Modi to the primary school in Vadnagar, where all the Modi children began their schooling. Narendra studied at this primary school from 1957 to 1964. During this period, his mother closely monitored him. As some of his teachers lived in Vadnagar, they gave his mother regular updates on his studies and mischievous antics.

Maa Heeraben and Narendra

I visited Narendra Modi's primary school during my stay in Vadnagar. The Archaeological Survey of India has been maintaining the school's upkeep since 2018. A two-storey building established in 1888, the school reverberates with the clamour of children. A room where Narendra Modi studied had benches arranged in rows.

I met Kanhaiyalal, Narendra Modi's third-grade teacher, who shared many stories about young Narendra and his mother. He mentioned one steadfast habit of Narendra Modi: his refusal to accept wrongdoing. Heeraben taught him to follow the right path from a young age. Kanhaiyalal said, 'Narendra's thinking was very clear at a very young age. I have not seen people with such clear thinking at such a young age before. Narendra understood the power of unity and knew how to bring people together.'

I also met Yogesh Shah, who was Narendra Modi's senior in school and now runs a clinic in Vadnagar. He said that the Modi family shared a good relationship with him, and their families often visited each other. He shared a childhood story about Modi: a teacher named Chandrashekhar Vyas beat a student in Narendra's class in front of fifty other students. This left a lasting impact

From Birth to School

on young Narendra, who recounted it entirely to Yogesh and his other classmates, many of whom were from Vadnagar. They decided to report this incident to the principal to ensure the teacher was not allowed back into the classroom and they gathered the support of many students from other classes. The principal assured the protesting students that this would not be repeated.

This incident occurred sixty or sixty-five years ago, but Yogesh recounted it with such clarity as though it had taken place yesterday. I was struck by the realisation that Modi understood the importance of truth at such an impressionable age. This was also because Heeraben taught him to live truthfully. This reflected the way she brought up her children, constantly imparting the difference between right and wrong, which helped her son navigate challenges in his adult life. During one of my conversations with her, when I asked about Modi's childhood, she said, 'Narendra never used to think about doing wrong.' Heeraben's eyes sparkled every time she talked about Narendra Modi, channelling immense self-confidence.

Narendra Modi's childhood was like that of any other child, but it was his thinking that was extraordinary. He took a keen interest in games like kho kho, kabaddi, cricket, kite-flying, wrestling and swimming. Swimming in the local pond was his preferred exercise for physical strength.

Just like every parent who recognises their children's abilities, Heeraben also knew that Narendra was skilled at bringing people together for a cause. Thus whenever she needed help with any job requiring the efforts of many people, he was entrusted to get the task done.

After working so closely with the prime minister for many years, I can vouch that talent and capability drive one to progress. During my visits to Vadnagar, Visnagar and Ahmedabad, I met many people and heard countless stories about him and gathered insights into the man he was before he became prime minister. Narendra Modi's approach to daily chores, like washing clothes, was also different and it attracted the attention of the villagers. He actively voiced his opinion against injustice at school, often informing the principal and prompting him to act against the culprits. His ability to disagree with elders without disrespecting them at home set him apart from his siblings, alerting Heeraben to his extraordinary abilities.

From Birth to School

The world knows about the special relationship Heeraben and Narendra shared, as Narendra Modi would often take time from his busy schedule to meet her. A mother usually calls her child constantly, reminds them to eat, worries about their academics and stays up all night watching over them when they fall sick. In a mother's presence, we never think about what life will be like without her, although eventually we must learn to live without her. For Modi too, his mother's death has left a void that may never be filled.

On his mother's birth centenary, Modi said in an article:

> Mother isn't just a word; she's an emotion of life in which there's affection, patience, faith and who knows how much more is contained. A mother doesn't just shape our bodies. Instead, she builds our minds, our personalities and our self-confidence, sacrificing herself for her children, forgetting herself. Today, whatever good is in my life, in my personality, is a gift from my mother and father. My mother is as ordinary as she is extraordinary.

Just like every mother. A mother's dedication makes her child a good human being. A mother's affection fills her child with humane emotions. A mother is not just a person; she is a form. Above every tale of absence is a mother's story of pride. Beyond every moment of struggle, there is the power of a mother's desire.

Former President A.P.J. Abdul Kalam wrote in his autobiography *Wings of Fire*:

Our mothers spend their lives day and night raising children, taking care of the household and sacrificing and working hard. One day, all of us siblings were eating together. Mother kept serving me rotis one after another. When I finished eating, my brother called me and scolded, 'Kalam, do you know what was happening? You were just eating roti after roti, and Mother kept giving them to you one by one. She even gave you all the rotis from her share. Times are tough at home right now. Be a sensible son and don't let Mother go hungry.' Hearing this, I trembled, ran to my mother, and hugged her.[1]

From Birth to School

Narendra Modi watched Heeraben do all her chores independently without asking for any help. She never asked her children to compromise on their studies to assist her with household chores. Modi highlighted this habit in an article about Heeraben written on his blog, 'Mother never expected us siblings to abandon our studies to help her.' His mother's struggles continued to inspire Modi well into his adult life and decision-making, for one never forgets the lessons learned during childhood.

I met Heeraben and Pankaj Modi in Ahmedabad and sat with them for several hours. Heeraben told me how Modi was during his childhood – his virtues, uniqueness and pranks. I tried to learn and understand how Heeraben taught, guided and educated her children, especially Narendra Modi. She was among the first people to recognise his instinct and skills for leadership during his childhood. For example, Narendra Modi had a damaged school wall rebuilt by collecting donations, which confirmed Heeraben's belief in his leadership abilities. Heeraben always supported Modi and showed unwavering faith in him. Narendra Modi's opinion was always taken into consideration when making a significant decision or undertaking a big task at home. He was inspired to think and act differently from others because of his mother's faith in him.

7

Deities, Faith and Belief

According to the Bhagavad Gita, there are no limits to God. Everything in this universe is born from God. God has no form, no shape, no beginning and no end. All living beings, rivers, mountains and everything else have originated from God.

Narendra Modi writes in his blog, 'Mother has deep faith in God, but she has always stayed far away from superstition. She has always protected our home from superstitions. She started off as a follower of the Kabir Panth and still performs worship according to that tradition… My mother has developed a habit of reciting prayers on a rosary.' Heeraben's children had to hide her rosary at night, or she would stay up late into the night praying.

Modi writes in his blog about his mother's acceptance of different opinions:

Maa Heeraben and Narendra

Once, near our house, a great saint was performing penance by cultivating wheat. I was deeply involved in serving him. During that time, my mother's sister, my aunt, was getting married. Everyone in the family had to go to my uncle's house, so my mother was also very excited. But when I went to my mother and told her that I did not want to go to my aunt's wedding, she asked for the reason. I told her about my conversation with the saint. My mother was saddened by this, but she respected my decision. My mother believed in and worshipped deities of all religions. She worshipped Maa Durga during Navratri, performed daily prayers, and never forgot to perform a havan.

Narendra Modi, like his mother, did not discriminate against followers of any religion, whether they were ascetics, sannyasis or faqirs. Narendra Modi writes in his blog:

Mother was very disciplined about time. She used to wake up at four in the morning and finish a lot of work. Whether it was grinding wheat or husking rice and lentils, she used

Deities, Faith and Belief

to do all the work herself. There is a famous hymn by Narasimha Mehta, '*Jal Kamal Chhandi Jane Vala, Swami Amaro Jagse*', and also a lullaby '*Shivaji Nu Halaradu*'. My mother used to hum both of them.

Heeraben's immense faith in God influenced Narendra Modi from childhood. He enjoyed playing characters in dramas who displayed leadership and acts of bravery. Heeraben played a significant role in developing this particular trait in Narendra, which helped cultivate leadership qualities from his childhood.

In addition to drawing inspiration from his mother, Narendra Modi was influenced by his father too. He wrote about his father in his blog: 'No matter the season – whether it was summer or monsoon – Father would wake up at four in the morning. People around could tell from the sound of his footsteps that it was four o'clock and Damodar Uncle was going to the temple. Going to the temple after leaving home and having a glimpse of the Lord was his daily routine.'

It is said, 'Devotion is attractive; it draws a person close to the Lord.' When a person dares to dive deep into a swimming pool, shaking with fear on the springboard, struggling for breath, and emerging victorious after the dive, the outside world begins to appear more radiant to them. The path to knowing the truth may be shown by God, but walking on it is a journey one must undertake oneself. Damodar Das Modi also guided young Narendra Modi on this path to success. Pankaj Modi explained, 'Father entrusted a very important task to young Narendra related to the Sharmistha pond. Every day, Narendra would spend hours bathing with friends in Vadnagar. There was no fixed time for him to return home. Father thought of assigning him the responsibility of serving the cow and entrusted Narendra with the duty of bathing and bringing the cow back home.'

Young Narendra Modi cared for the cow with great affection, becoming a gau sevak at a very early age. Additionally, he understood the importance of working in groups and would often ask for help from his friends in the gau seva assigned by his father. For example, while bathing the cows, one friend would massage the cow's back, another would rub its forehead and yet another would rub the cow with a cloth. Though these acts seem ordinary, they become extraordinary when performed with thoughtfulness and attention. Narendra Modi made every task unique through his skills.

Modi says, 'In my mother there was a great quality – compassion towards every living being. This was evident in her behaviour. During the hot days, she always kept grains and water in earthen pots for the birds.' Once, Home Minister Amit Shah shared an interesting story about Prime Minister Narendra Modi. Modi was conducting an important meeting at his residence on Lok Kalyan Marg when a peacock began striking its beak loudly against the recently installed glass. As soon as Narendra Modi saw the peacock, he paused the meeting and said, 'Oh, I forgot to provide food and water [for] it due to the meeting.'

Narendra Modi, in an article about his mother, said:

There were stray dogs in the alleys around my home; my mother took care that they did not go hungry. We also had rights over the neighbourhood cows. Every day, my mother would feed the cow with roti. Not dry roti, but always roti smeared with ghee. Whenever sadhus or saints visited our home, my mother would ensure they had a meal, and when they were about to leave, she wouldn't ask for herself but would request for my siblings and me, 'Bless my children that they see joy in others' happiness and sorrow in their sorrows. May my children always maintain devotion and a spirit of service...' My mother used to seek this blessing.

During my conversations with Heeraben, she spoke of the divine grace that blesses their family. Narendra Modi has also mentioned visiting Kedarnath and Badrinath with Heeraben. During one of their visits, the cold intensified and she lacked sufficient clothing. Narendra Modi instantly alerted the group he was working with, prompting immediate assistance for her. Heeraben believed that Narendra's exemplary feats attracted this support.

The entire Modi family was deeply religious, with immense faith in God. Heeraben regularly observed Chaturmasa, a four-month spiritual retreat where people observe fasts for up to sixteen days, read scriptures, practise yoga and donate to charity. In his blog, Modi writes:

> It was in 2017 when I was in Kashi during the last days of the UP elections. I had brought prasad for Mother from Kashi when I went to Ahmedabad. Mother asked if I had seen Kashi Vishwanath Mahadev. Mother always says the full name – Kashi Vishwanath Mahadev. Then, during the conversation, Mother asked if the way to Kashi Vishwanath Mahadev temple is still the same. It feels like a temple has been built in someone's home. When I was surprised and asked her when she had gone there, Mother told me she had gone many years ago.

The poet and playwright Jaishankar Prasad writes, 'Where our beautiful imagination rests by making a nest of ideals, that is heaven. That is the place of recreation and love. Heaven is found in this world only. Whoever did not find it is unfortunate in this world.'

The Chinese philosopher and poet Laozi contends, 'There is neither a prior imagination

Maa Heeraben and Narendra

of heaven nor earth. A wise person does not distinguish, he sees all humans as holy objects created for sacred use. There is nothing solid in the celestial sphere, but it never collapses at any time. There is nothing better than self-restraint.'

Much like a wise person who remains indifferent to their own self-interest, the soul remains resilient in dealing with life's hardships. Such people are invested in the welfare of others more than in themselves.

Narendra Modi displayed qualities of altruism from childhood, a trait he learned from his mother. The Modi children received money to spend at the village fairs held around festivals. During the 1963 Bihar floods, Narendra Modi and his friends wanted to use their fair money to provide aid to the flood victims. Narendra's childhood friend Ishwar Bhai Patel recalls, 'We decided to sell tea at the fair. Narendra was assigned the responsibility of making tea because he made it the best. The reason for this was that he knew how long to boil the tea and at what temperature from working at the stall with his father. A tea stall was set up at the fair. For this, we gathered a stove, a large pot and all the equipment needed to make tea from our home. Tea started brewing at the fair, and all of us started filling it in kettles to sell. We earned a good amount from this and gathered more than seven hundred rupees and gave it to Dr Basant Parikh, who was working to provide relief materials around Vadnagar during the Bihar floods.' This example deftly depicts Narendra Modi's leadership skills.

8

Father's Teachings

During a rally in Aligarh, Prime Minister Narendra Modi shared a story from his childhood:

> This incident took place fifty-five to sixty years ago. Salesmen who sold locks in Aligarh used to come to my village [Vadnagar]. I remember they wore black jackets. As salesmen, they would leave locks at shops and return after three months to collect the money. They also used to visit neighbouring businessmen in our village and sell locks to them. My father had a good friendship with them. Whenever they came, they would stay in our village for five to six days. After collecting money all day, they would leave the amount with my father. My father would keep track of this money. Four

to six days later, when they left the village, they would take all the money with them by train. I heard and saw this in my childhood.'

These childhood lessons helped Narendra Modi differentiate the good from the bad and showed him the right path.

A video was uploaded on the website of the Prime Minister's Office in memory of Heeraben, in which Narendra Modi said, 'Respected Mother! You and I are connected by a thread of blessings. Just as a door in the vast cosmos binds a space traveller to himself, it does not let go. Your blessings are like that thread. Your values should always remain, sometimes as protectors and sometimes as guides.'

The values and lessons of brotherhood and impartiality taught to the Modi children were evident when I met Pankaj Modi in Ahmedabad. Kahlil Gibran says, 'There are those who have little and give it all. These are the believers in life and the bounty of life, and their coffer is never empty.' The Modi family too believed in this philosophy, for they lacked abundance but were content, largely because of Damodar Das's thinking. Pankaj Modi shared a story: 'Near

Father's Teachings

Vadnagar, there was a village named Kesimpa. There lived a Miyan Bhai with his children. Miyan Bhai's son's name was Abbas. Only education up to class seven was available in Kesimpa. One day, Miyan Bhai came to meet my parents from Kesimpa and shared his problems. "Let me tell you, brother, that my son Abbas is very bright in studies. There is no secondary school in our village, and I worry that my son's education might suffer." Heeraben and Damodar Das said, "Don't worry about Abbas's education; send him to our house. Abbas will study at our home. Pankaj and Abbas will study together."' Heeraben provided Abbas with meals and support despite the Modis' financial struggle. This incident highlights the family's hospitality, which extended beyond caste and religion.

Narendra Modi has also shared this story in his blog. He writes, 'In a way, Abbas stayed in our house during his childhood studies. Like the other children in the house, Mother took very good care of Abbas too. On Eid, Mother used to prepare his favourite dishes for Abbas... Mother always remained happy seeing others happy. Although there was little space at home, her heart was very big.[2]

Maa Heeraben and Narendra

Abbas now lives in Sydney, Australia. When the story came out, Vishal Pandey, a journalist working with Zee News, travelled to Australia to get a statement from him. I talked to him at length about Abbas. Pandey quoted Abbas as saying, 'I am from Kesimpa village, which is four kilometres away from Modi's village Vadnagar. Kesimpa falls under the Gaikwad State. My father and Damodar Kaka were very good friends. I completed my eleventh grade there. I lived with the Modi family just like any other family member. Whenever there was a festival, I was a part of the rituals. Heeraben used to make special dishes for me. If my clothes got dirty, Heeraben would even ask for them to be washed.'

I too had a long conversation with Abbas, who lives as a member of the Damodar Das Modi family in Australia, which helped me understand Heeraben and her motherhood even more deeply. Though this is a story from many years ago, Heeraben's treating Abbas as her own child portrays her greatness.

9

Heeraben's Concerns

Heeraben was always anxious about Narendra Modi. Modi writes in his book *Sakshi Bhav*:

> Seeing the time when the boy returns home from school and waiting, how much visible restlessness is reflected in a mother's eyes. Feet hustle in and out. After continuous efforts to look around, the bustling of the street doesn't appear; her eyes search for her child, her ears eagerly await to hear the word 'mother', and if there's even a moment's delay, the heartbeat shakes the walls, the feet move restlessly, the eyes are petrified with anxieties, and the pain of separation begins to flow.

Heeraben was very proud of Narendra Modi since his childhood and would ask ascetics and sages about his future. In *The Real Modi* I wrote about an incident from 1963 when Narendra Modi was thirteen.[1] It was customary for the locals to host visiting ascetics in Vadnagar. One such ascetic visited the Modi house for a meal and requested the family's birth charts. Heeraben gave him her eldest child Somnath's chart along with Narendra Modi's.

Upon examining the elder child's birth chart, the ascetic said, 'His life will be ordinary, but there is a chance he will go to jail once.' When the ascetic looked at Narendra Modi's birth chart, his eyes widened. He asked, 'Whose birth chart is this?' Heeraben replied, 'This is my third son Narendra's birth chart. Why do you ask? Is everything okay?' The ascetic said, 'This is a very influential birth chart. If this boy goes into politics, his influence will spread like an emperor, and if he becomes an ascetic, he will assume a position like a Shankaracharya.'

During my Vadnagar trip, I met two childhood friends of Narendra Modi who shared insights about him. Shyamlal Das Madhavlal recalled, 'This incident happened when Narendra Modi was in the fifth grade. At that time, both of us asked an astrologer about our future. The astrologer said that vehicles will revolve under Narendra Modi.'

It is generally beautiful to get lost in the past, but one gets entangled in the hardships of life through daily struggles. The Modi family also faced challenges, and Narendra Modi's life was filled with obstacles. Heeraben worried that Narendra would want to do different things in life and explore new paths, which might create distance between the two of them. She recounted, 'He was always different from others since childhood; his perspective on every task or subject was completely unique, and he never hesitated to express himself.'

When I asked Narendra Modi's sister, Basanti, about their parents' views of him since childhood, she said, 'Father always wanted Narendra Bhai to study and achieve something so that the family's days of sorrow would end, because among all the siblings, Narendra Bhai was the most intelligent. Sometimes Father would get very upset about this.' Basanti added that Heeraben was extremely supportive of Narendra Modi and believed he had a unique talent for improving things.

In *Narendra Modi: A Political Biography*, Andy Marino recalls that when he asked Narendra

Maa Heeraben and Narendra

Modi about his childhood, Modi smiled and said, 'Innovation, new ideas, that was basically my temperament.'[2] Narendra Modi was a curious and eager child with great leadership skills.

Narendra Modi's instinct to lead and innovate in dire situations helped him achieve remarkable things at a very young age. Ishwar Bhai Patel and Sudhir Joshi, who studied with Narendra Modi, shared a noteworthy story. Sudhir recalled, 'The wall of our B.N. High School collapsed, disrupting our studies. Narendra was in eighth grade then.' Ishwar added, 'We decided to rebuild the wall and asked people for donations. Our group came together to make it happen. We organised a fundraiser and staged a play at the school which helped us collect funds. Our team met with respected community members to discuss methods to raise money, and they offered to assist us. The play helped us enough economically and the wall was rebuilt successfully.' Thus, Narendra Modi's attempts to take initiative and his investment in the work were extraordinary. Heeraben not only watched over him but also guided him throughout his journey to help others.

Heeraben and son Narendra share some loving moments

10

Family Livelihood and Parental Imparting: A Boon for Politics

Heeraben and Damodar Das Modi played equally important roles in Narendra Modi's upbringing. Modi wrote in his blog, 'Our family was a joint family, and both parents worked equally hard to run the household cart.'

Narendra Modi has often mentioned in his speeches that he sold tea at Vadnagar railway station. In an interview with the actor Akshay Kumar,[1] Modi revealed that selling tea on trains provided him with an opportunity to understand people, as some scolded him while others explained certain things. The prime minister said, 'Sometimes businessmen from Mumbai came by goods train and we served them tea and had conversations with them. I learned

Hindi through these conversations.' Modi has often recounted how his mother used to spin the charkha and sew clothes to contribute to household finances. Narendra Modi witnessed his mother's daily struggles, and this motivated him to work at the tea stall with his father in his extra time.

In *Narendra Modi*, Andy Marino writes that Modi was always eager to help out wherever he could. 'After school, Narendra would race to his father's tea stall as if working there was the excitement he had been looking forward to all day long and nothing in the world was more fulfilling than serving tea to railway passengers ...'[2]

When Narendra Modi was admitted to the RSS office, his skill in making tea provided him with a stable position and helped him in his political journey. Prem Chand Koder Bhai Patel, who worked with Narendra Modi at the Gujarat chief minister's office, told me, 'When Narendra Modi was assigned the responsibility of making tea in the Sangh [RSS] office in the early days, I was appointed his assistant – my role was to grind ginger for tea, clean the tea utensils and serve tea to the Sangh leaders or workers who came from outside.' Thus, the Modi family's livelihood along

Family Livelihood and Parental Imparting

with the work taught by his parents became a political boon for Narendra Modi in his career, whether in volunteer work or in becoming a leader.

When I met Narendra Modi, the topic of railways naturally came up. He told me about the different experiences and opportunities his tea-selling job provided him. Modi recalled a polio-stricken twelve- or thirteen-year-old boy who used to polish the shoes of passengers on trains. When Modi first saw him, he was struggling to board a train. The boy requested passengers for a chance to polish their shoes — in those days shoe polishing cost about ten or fifteen paise. Narendra Modi said, 'I had seen many shoe polishers, but this one was different. Once he pulled out a newspaper from his worn-out bag with the words, "May your day be auspicious. May your journey be successful. May your work be accomplished." He gave his customers a newspaper to read for ten paise. Curious, I asked him where he was from, and he replied that he was from Karnataka and had no family. He wanted to live with dignity and serve others.' This incident had a lasting impact on Narendra Modi, which also resonates with the teachings of the Bhagavad Gita that exhorts people to perform their duties without attachment to the outcome. You have to do your duty to the best of your ability, always mindful that the results of your work will depend on many factors. Modi never forgot the young boy even when he became the prime minister.

In the book *Social Harmony*, Kishor Makwana highlights Narendra Modi's speech on social security and the assistance provided by the government when he was the chief minister of Gujarat.[3] Modi says, 'Gujarat is the first state that has taken upon itself the responsibility of insuring unorganised labourers. The government contributes to their insurance.' A significant reason behind Narendra Modi's insurance schemes for the poor was his memories of the time his father was struck with bone marrow cancer and the family's struggles to pay the hospital bills. Narendra Modi launched the Ayushman Bharat scheme in 2018 enabling patients from any economic background to receive medical treatment in hospitals across the country.

During the inauguration of the Jan Dhan Yojana in New Delhi on 28 August 2014, Narendra Modi remarked, 'It is a matter of joy that many records are being broken today. Perhaps never before in history has insurance for accidents been provided to one and a half crore people in one day. This is a huge record. Despite political benefits, those who witness others in pain step forward to help as I have seen since my childhood. Today, the number of Jan Dhan accounts has crossed fifty crore.'

Narendra Modi was extremely happy that more than half of the Jan Dhan accounts were in the name of women, which meant that almost 56 per cent of the accounts were opened by them. Of these, 67 per cent were opened in rural and semi-urban areas. According to a finance ministry report in 2024, the total deposit amount in Jan Dhan accounts exceeds ₹2.03 lakh crore. Thirty-four crore cards have been issued, free of cost, from these accounts.

Narendra Modi, first as chief minister and then as prime minister, ensured that the problems and hardships witnessed by him and his family would not be experienced by the people of the country. His struggles, the family's financial hardships and the challenges of his father fighting bone marrow cancer always inspired Narendra Modi to work differently from others for the nation.

11

Prayers Answered

Heeraben's faith in God was unwavering. She believed there was a path and a plan for everyone's life and this depended on the grace of God. Always carrying a tulsi mala in her hand, Heeraben constantly chanted the name of God. Modi once recalled in his article how she would sometimes get so absorbed in chanting that she would even forget to sleep. To ensure that she got the necessary rest, the mala often had to be hidden away.

When I met Heeraben in Ahmedabad, she appeared like a saint in a white sari. Devoid of ornamentation, her self-assuredness was reflected in her eyes. The room too was sparse – a photograph of a guru hung on one wall and an idol of God was kept across from it. There was a TV in one corner for Heeraben to religiously watch her son Narendra during his public appearances. A copy of the Bhagavad Gita was also kept nearby, a reminder of the lesson that, in a way, defined the lives of her children: perform your duties without attachment to reaping its fruit (*karm karo parantu phal ki chinta na karo*).

In their village, Pankaj Modi told me, a Bhagavad Katha was held in the month of Shravana each year. Everyone was invited to attend it. Transported back to the days of his childhood in Vadnagar, he remembered how once his mother waited for him at the katha to bring her flowers. She waited for a very long time until she got some flowers through another person and the katha began with her son nowhere in sight.

Pankaj had plucked the flowers as per her instructions and was on his way to the recital at Paramanand Gandhi's house when he made a stop at the study centre nearby. No longer functional, it had been established in the 1960s and run by the Swadhyaya family, whose many centres were based on the teachings of the Gita. Distracted by the activities at the centre, Pankaj forgot all about the katha and his mother.

Prayers Answered

By the time he remembered that he had to take the flowers to Heeraben, it was too late. He reached home nervous, expecting admonishments from his family members. He had to hear an earful for his recklessness, and no one believed him when he told them where he had been held up. 'At the time, only one person supported me, and that was Narendra Modi,' Pankaj said. Modi encouraged his younger brother to go to the centre regularly.

Many such important decisions in the family were taken by Modi, explained Pankaj Modi and his sister, Basanti. His mother loved him the most, and with her standing in front of him like a shield, who could refuse him anything? He weighed everything meticulously before arriving at any conclusion. He relied on traditions and disliked deceit. In the Modi household, Narendra's word prevailed.

During our conversation, Pankaj quietly made tea for me. As I drank it, Heeraben said something to him in Gujarati. From the bits and pieces that I could understand I gathered that she wanted him to tell me how Narendra had once spent the money he earned at a fair on public service. I smiled at her eagerness to ensure that none of her son's virtues went unrecognised.

After that she slowly sipped her tea from the steel glass, her eyes glued to the television which showed the prime minister of India speaking in the United States. Heeraben's face beamed with pride as she took in the scene. It was perhaps inspired by the realisation that her son was successfully marching on the path he had chosen for himself.

12

It Starts at Home

Under the influence of his parents, Narendra's relentless spirit began to take shape, with faith, courage and a sense of selflessness forming the core elements of his personality. Encouraged by his mother and inspired by the teachings of his father, Narendra was determined to achieve all the goals he set his heart on. During his growing-up years, he seemed to live by Kahlil Gibran's maxim: 'Your daily life is your temple and your religion. When you enter into it take with you your all.'

Often when his family members couldn't find him in the village, their first guess was that he would be at the Vadnagar library. Both Pankaj Modi and Basanti Ben fondly remembered how their brother enjoyed reading books about great men. From early on, he wanted to learn and imbibe the qualities of honourable persons, including his mother and father, whom he held in great reverence.

Narendra Modi was eight years old when he joined the Rashtriya Swayamsevak Sangh branch in Vadnagar. When I met Heeraben in Ahmedabad, I wanted her views on what had prompted her son to take this step. She had a very brief answer. With her eyes still fixed on her son on the TV, she said, 'He had always been like that. He was always inclined towards serving people, helping them through their sorrows and pains...' I asked his friends and teachers the same question. Sudhir Joshi, Narendra's friend from school, who runs a dispensary in Vadnagar, told me, 'Narendra Modi and his family have experienced a lot of poverty. It was his and his family's desire to liberate themselves and other families from poverty.' It was perhaps this that drove Modi to choose the RSS and do his part for the betterment of others.

In Ahmedabad, Narendra Modi's friend Dr Anil Raval related an experience from Modi's life as an RSS volunteer that crystallised his ambition to work towards the eradication of poverty in the country. During those days in the early 1960s, the RSS provided morning tea and snacks to its volunteers, who were generally offered meals at the homes they visited or they made do with offerings to God (prasad) in the evening. RSS volunteers go door to door for outreach work; they had to combed through villages and cities to spread their message and did not have a permanent place to stay.

So it happened that a twelve-year-old Narendra was hosted by the family of a poor, disabled man. 'His dhoti was clean but torn on one side. The enthusiasm with which he hugged me dispelled all my tiredness,' Modi later recounted to Anil Raval. For dinner he was served a pearl millet roti and a small bowl of milk. As he was about to eat, he noticed the couple's five-year-old son eyeing the milk. Realising that perhaps the family was feeding him a share of their son's food, he felt immensely guilty. He gave the milk to the child, who drank it quickly. He was touched by the sacrifice of the mother and father and in that moment resolved to devote his life to alleviating the suffering of others.

The year was 1962 when India lost the war with China and the defeat deeply affected the Indian polity and its people. Narendra Modi was regularly attending RSS meetings during this time, where he was taught lessons of patriotism and stories of brave figures like Shivaji. Against this backdrop, Narendra was inspired to study in a military school, but poverty and life's practicalities stood in the way of that dream.

When he was fifteen, the country witnessed another border conflict. Vadnagar was on the supply line of the 1965 India–Pakistan war. Soldiers would pass through this route and sometimes return injured. An adolescent Modi served tea to the soldiers for free. Given that his family was struggling to earn their daily bread and make ends meet, serving free tea was no small sacrifice. Narendra Modi had found his purpose in the path of patriotism and selfless service.

13

Blessings and Counsel

Narendra Modi lived the life of a nomad. He was never permanently settled at home. On meeting Heeraben, I asked her if in her heart she ever wanted to stop her son from leaving his mother behind, to which she replied, 'He never did anything wrong, whether it was making decisions at home or outside. So I let him make his own choices.'

Shortly before 1966, when the Gujarat State Transport Corporation hiked ticket prices, Narendra started a job at his uncle Babu Bhai's small canteen near the State Transport Office. When members of the Jan Sangh joined a protest near Geeta Mandir, the frail young man accompanied them in chanting slogans against the price hike. He carried a placard displaying a picture of Deendayal Upadhyaya. That was when the protest's organiser,

Maa Heeraben and Narendra

Ambalal Koshi, spotted him and discovered that he was merely sixteen years old and earned his living by working at a tea shop.

Soon after, at Hedgewar Bhavan, the Sangh headquarters, Narendra met Lakshmanrao Inamdar, whom he has acknowledged as his political mentor. He spent over a year living in a small room at Hedgewar Bhavan, where he worked from early morning till late at night, making tea, serving breakfast, sweeping and mopping the rooms, and visiting volunteers' homes. He had skilfully devoted himself to his mentor and to the Sangh.

At the age of seventeen, Narendra Modi made a big decision. Faced with the challenges of adolescence – trying to find answers to the questions about the world that constantly arose in his mind and reconcile with society and traditional life around him – he took a big step. On 3 June 1967, the young man left his home, family and education behind for two years.

In Ahmedabad I tried to learn from all members of the Modi family the reasons that drove the seventeen-year-old to purposefully abandon the comforts of home. After all, leaving loved ones is never easy. His decision had shaken both his parents, but his mother still stood by him. His brother Soma Modi maintains that Narendra wanted to leave home but not by running away; he wanted to do so with the blessings of his elders. According to his sister, while Damodar Das Modi was not supportive of his son's decision, he accepted it. Finally, 3 June was chosen as the day of his departure. His mother prepared a special meal, and they all ate together as if celebrating a festival. Then, Narendra Modi set out on his solitary journey.

He had very little in the way of belongings. He had few clothes and only a small amount of money that he had saved from selling cans of cooking oil for local merchants. Andy Marino quotes Narendra Modi in his book *Narendra Modi* as saying: 'There was no comfort in my life. I had a small bag and my whole life was in that bag.'[1]

There was no destination to this journey. Its purpose was to acquaint young Narendra with the world and to teach him endurance in the face of adversity. His pockets were empty, but he was led by the pursuit of life experiences and wisdom. He headed towards West Bengal and in the summer of 1968 reached Belur Math, the headquarters of the Ramakrishna Math and Ramakrishna

Mission. Situated on the western bank of the Hooghly River, the math was then headed by its president Swami Madhavananda Ji Maharaj. He stayed there for a week and roamed in and around Calcutta before heading to the Ramakrishna Math in Guwahati. And then to the Ramakrishna Math in the Himalayan foothills near Almora, from where he embarked on a forty-day trek.

Narendra Modi eventually arrived at the Ramakrishna Ashram in Rajkot. There he entertained the idea of becoming a monk and living a life of austerity, not much different from how he lived during his travels, but fate had other plans. Swami Atmasthananda advised him to let go of that dream, for he assessed that Narendra was fundamentally not suited to become a monk. He told him that his destiny lay elsewhere and that he should continue on the path he was on to seek it.

An understanding of truth cannot happen without the silence of solitude. In a TV interview with Rajeev Shukla, Modi said that being alone on his travels had given him great satisfaction. This journey had shown him all seasons and the many colours of life. His spirit had hardened; he was steadfast and resolute now – qualities that he further refined during the rise of his political career.

Blessings and Counsel

In early 1970, Narendra Modi returned home. He informed no one of his arrival. His mother was cooking when he entered the house. His sister remembers screaming in joy, 'Bhai is back, bhai is back!' Hearing this, their mother came running from the kitchen. She forgot all her worries, all her concerns upon seeing him. She inquired about his health, where he had been and why he looked so weak. Then she lovingly fed him while asking him a myriad of questions, some of which he refused to answer. He left for the village soon after finishing his meal.

Heeraben noticed that his bag contained only a pair of clothes, a saffron-coloured shawl and one photo. She was touched and surprised to see that he had carried her photo with him wherever he went. She had no clue how or from where he had procured that photograph.

14

Catalyst for Tomorrow

As the country experienced great transformations in the 1970s, so too did Narendra Modi. The decade tested his dedication to the cause of the country, the outcome of which catapulted his political career in the direction of great success. By the time the country came under the twenty-one-month-long Emergency imposed in 1975, Narendra Modi had become a valued worker for the Rashtriya Swayamsevak Sangh.

While he had already gained the faith and trust of Lakshmanrao Inamdar, he gradually proved his worth to the other members of the Sangh as well, especially by participating in the Sangh's struggle against the Emergency. In Navsari, senior Sangh worker Kanti Bhai Vyas mentioned how Narendra Modi also went into hiding after arrest warrants were issued against members of the Sangh. However, he continued to work for the organisation by engaging in underground activities. Then twenty-five years old, Modi worked extensively in Gujarat, where the anti-Emergency movement was active in Vadodara, Rajkot and Ahmedabad.

Prakash Mehta, another Sangh worker, recalls how Narendra would randomly come knocking at his door to entrust him with a task, sometimes even in the middle of the night. Once he asked him to drop off a person at an unknown location on a scooter. Mehta was not told the person's name, and he did not ask any questions. Mehta says, 'A month later, I found out that the person I had dropped was Dattopant Thengadi, who was a member of the Rajya Sabha from the Bharatiya Jana Sangh.'

Modi also worked towards looking after the families of Sangh members who were imprisoned. Rajan Daya Bhai Bhatt, an old Sangh worker from Valsad, remembers Narendra Modi for helping his family when his father went underground. Lalita Ben Ojha, a Sangh worker from Vadodara, gratefully recounts how he went to great lengths to take care of her family. 'During the Emergency days my father was in jail for fourteen months.

Narendra Modi used to visit us every other day and take care of us and all our needs, ensuring we had enough food at home,' she said.

While he took care of other people's families, their mothers and their children, his own mother worried for him in Vadnagar. With most of the Sangh leaders and workers in prison, all Sangh members and participants in the anti-Emergency movement faced the danger of being arrested. Receiving hardly any word from her son about his whereabouts, she spent her days in distress. Reflecting on this time in his life, Modi has written, 'A devotee's ardent call is to his reverend mother... Mother is my expectation, the fulfilment of the Self. Mother is my expectation, the endless expansion of my uniqueness. Mother is my expectation to become myself...'

Finally, a time came when she could no longer wait to see him. But arranging a meeting wasn't that simple, until Uncle Babu Bhai Modi came to their rescue. Pankaj Modi, who worked at *Hindustan Samachar* in Ahmedabad, received a message at his office one day, asking him to take his parents to their uncle's house. 'I'll come there at nine in the morning, the message had read,' Pankaj recounted. With a glimmer of hope, the mother and father started preparing for the meeting, and they reached Babu Bhai's house long before nine on the designated day.

'Exactly at nine, a Sikh gentleman arrived. Narendra Bhai came in disguise so that no one would recognise him... I still remember tears rolling down Mother's face when she saw him,' Pankaj Modi recalled.

Narendra Modi stepped forward and greeted his mother, who had long been waiting to see her son again. She was relieved to see him, to hear him speak. According to Pankaj Modi, after Narendra Modi explained that all this was being done for Bharat Mata, Heeraben and Damodar Das Modi were reassured that their son was on the right track. Yes, they feared for their son's safety, but they knew the cause was important to him and nothing would stop him. They blessed him and asked him to take care of himself. Heeraben bid him farewell as he prepared to leave his uncle's house. She prayed for his well-being and wished him luck. But, above all, she wondered when she would see her son again.

15

Narendra's Asceticism, Mother's Support

'The steadfast person who can control the senses gains knowledge; that knowledge leads them toward the highest peace.'

                              Bhagavad Gita

On 22 January 2024, Ayodhya saw a grand inauguration of the Ram Mandir. Before the consecration of the temple, Prime Minister Modi observed a rigorous fast for eleven days. During the fast, he lived on fruits and coconut water and slept on the ground. People wondered how he was able to adhere to such a rigorous routine with such discipline. The answer lies in his younger years.

Maa Heeraben and Narendra

As Andy Marino writes in *Narendra Modi*, Narendra Modi always had a resourcefulness and intellectual hunger, which his mother recognised. Heeraben feared that one day her son would leave not just their home but the town – the entire world – behind. Her fears came true when, in 1967, Modi chose asceticism and set off across India, determined to gain knowledge and seek spiritual growth.

The Bhagavad Gita teaches that controlling one's senses leads to wisdom, and wisdom brings peace. Unlike many children who demand luxuries, Modi chose the path of discipline. He spent two years travelling across India, enduring heat, cold and hardship, living under the open sky. This journey marked the beginning of his quest for truth and self-understanding.

A similar journey was undertaken in 1891 by a young man named Narendra Nath Datta, who later came to be known as Swami Vivekananda. Rajendra Mohan Bhatnagar writes in his book *Vivekananda*, 'The journey that began in 1891 kept instructing him to move forward, never looking back. Infinite spiritual, social and mysterious experiences took hold of him so much that he often forgot himself.'

Narendra's Asceticism, Mother's Support

Narendra Modi, deeply influenced by Vivekananda's teachings, absorbed his spiritual wisdom during his own travels. For Modi, the two years away from home were devoid of worldly comfort, but they were formative, shaping his view of the world. The determination and discipline that saw Narendra Modi through those years of hardship can be seen in the succeeding years with every challenge he takes on. When Gujarat was grappling with consecutive droughts from 1985 to 1987, Modi exposed the government's incompetence to the public. During this period, three major incidents of communal riots occurred in Gujarat, with each riot resulting in more deaths than the previous one. To defuse the tension, the BJP organised roadshows and launched two statewide campaigns, in which Modi played a significant role behind the scenes. The first journey, conducted in 1987, was called the Nyay Yatra. The Nyay Yatra began in Gujarat in December 1987. This journey was to cover 15,000 villages across 115 districts. The second journey, conducted in 1989, was named the Lok Shakti Rath Yatra.

In 1989, Modi organised the Lok Shakti Rath Yatra, from planning the route to organising public meetings. The aim was to combat the liquor mafia that was wreaking havoc on society. Starting from the Ambaji Temple, this journey passed through 10,000 villages. Like everything Modi undertakes, this journey began with deep discipline. He believes that when a task is rooted in purity, self-discipline and spirituality, the journey to achieving it brings true joy.

During a conversation with Kishor Makwana, Narendra Modi says, 'When Lal Krishna Advani's Somanath–Ayodhya Rath Yatra began, I faced a tough test. I was responsible for organising the entire journey, and it coincided with Navratri. I only consumed water; I didn't eat or drink anything else. On the third day, when Advani Ji's wife Kamla Bhabhi learned that I was working without eating or drinking, tears welled up in her eyes.' Kamla Advani had told Narendra, 'Does Narendra Bhai run like this all the time? Give yourself some rest.' In response, Narendra had said that this was his life, and he found joy in it.

Modi's commitment to asceticism was also clear during the Kailash Manasarovar Yatra. He undertook this journey with twenty-six other people, all decked in saffron clothes. Throughout the trip, he maintained strict vows and used the

Narendra's Asceticism, Mother's Support

experience to deepen his spiritual knowledge, often teaching others in the group about the importance of the guru. Jayashree Bahen Trivedi, who was part of the group on the Kailash Manasarovar Yatra, recalls, 'We reached Kailash on Guru Purnima after a three-day journey. Narendra Bhai became famous in the group for his asceticism and vows. In Kailash, Narendra Bhai explained to all of us in the group the importance of the guru.'

His discipline extended to his daily life including his fasts during Navratri, which he observed even while travelling abroad. Modi told Kishor Makwana, author of *Modi: Common Man's PM*, 'I meditate for two hours. I practise pranayama, yoga and meditation every day. For many years, I have been worshipping Ambaji, venerating power.'

In September 2022, when I visited Heeraben and Pankaj Modi's home in Ahmedabad during Navratri, Modi was on a trip to the US. Even during his trip abroad, he adhered to the rules of the Navratri fast. Whether it was a dinner hosted by the US President or a royal banquet in honour of Prince William, he remained true to his principles. When I asked Heeraben about

Narendra Modi's commitment and determination, she told me, 'He has been like this since childhood - resolute and demonstrative.'

Heeraben, although sometimes worried about her son's extreme practices and urging him to ease up, always supported him. She would prepare special meals for the family when Narendra fasted. Even when his practices became more intense over the years, she never objected. Modi once wrote, 'My mother never complained about my experiments. She would just say, "Do as you wish, my son."'

Narendra Modi writes, 'Since she herself observed strict discipline regularly, she knew my rules during Navratri.' Modi was steadfast and did not waver from his fasting rules. It was a lesson taught by his mother in his childhood: to do every task with purity.

Heeraben always stood by her son, respecting his wishes. She always kept an eye on him, never letting Narendra become weak due to fasting. During his childhood, when Narendra observed fasts, Heeraben would prepare the day's fasting meal for the entire family, which everyone would eat, such as potatoes and onions and 'shikanji'.

Narendra's Asceticism, Mother's Support

Basanti Ben told me that very often Heeraben and Narendra would observe fasting and penance together. Even during elections, Narendra Modi never abandoned his commitment to discipline.

Before beginning his eleven-day austerity in January 2024, Modi tweeted: 'It is my fortune to witness the consecration of Ram Lalla in Ayodhya. Today, I begin my special austerity for 11 days. I seek the blessings of all people.' This tweet captured Modi's humility and reverence for the occasion, as well as his enduring commitment to his spiritual and national mission.[1]

16

Maa's Sense of Service and Home Remedies

Heeraben recognised that inner talent not only sets you apart from others but also earns respect and distinction in society. She believed in the power of service and love. Whenever someone visited her home, Heeraben made sure they left with help, no matter what. When I met Heeraben and Pankaj Modi in Ahmedabad, Pankaj shared with me the vast array of her skills and the impact of her service. He spoke of how she welcomed visitors with kindness. This profound generosity left a lasting impression on everyone. It shows that where there is love, there is service, and where service flourishes, love takes root. In India, where love and service are highly valued, Heeraben's eagerness to help those in need, despite her own poverty, was truly inspiring.

Maa Heeraben and Narendra

Pankaj Modi told me that Heeraben had a remarkable knowledge of home remedies and knew how to treat a myriad of illnesses. He shared some incredible details of Heeraben's contributions. He recalled how people used to gather at their home early every morning for home remedies. One of her specialties was treating ailments caused by a misaligned navel – such as nausea, dizziness, constipation and severe stomach pain. These issues, Pankaj explained, could also disrupt menstruation for women. Heeraben had a natural ability to diagnose and treat these conditions effectively.

The Modi family was not affluent by any means, but Heeraben had a generous heart. After finishing her morning chores, she would sit down and patiently listen to everyone's troubles, understand them and suggest solutions. Without fail she would send something to eat for the hungry patients, especially the children and the elderly. Pankaj said, 'Maa used to suggest very accurate home remedies. Most of the time, small children or the elderly faced problems like an itchy or sore throat, difficulty swallowing or a runny nose. Maa's touch had a magical effect; patients would recover with her touch.'

Maa's Sense of Service and Home Remedies

Narendra Modi wrote:

> My mother has as much sensitivity and a service-oriented nature as her piercing vision. Mother knows many traditional methods for treating young children. During the holidays in Vadnagar, there would often be long queues for treatment. People would come even to show 6- to 8-month-old babies. To prepare the medicine, Maa often needed a very fine powder. Collecting this powder was our responsibility as children of the house. Mother would tie a cloth tightly around the mouth of a bowl and grind 5–6 cloves. The ash from the stove was collected and sprinkled on the cloth, gradually rubbing it in. This process caused the finest particles of ash to accumulate in the bowl. Mother's instruction was always, 'Do your work well, so that the children don't face any problems due to the larger grains of ash.'

In this vein, Narendra Modi shared another memory:

> I recall another incident related to my mother's remedies and wisdom. Once, we had

to perform a religious ritual for my father. We all had to go to the banks of the Narmada for this purpose. It was terribly hot, so we set out early in the morning. The journey must have been about three to four hours. When we got off the bus, we had to walk further on foot. But the heat was so intense that it felt like fire was emanating from the ground. We started walking with our feet in the water at the edge of the Narmada. Walking in the river is not easy. After a short while, we children became terribly tired, and we were also very hungry. Mother asked Father to wait for a while and to fetch jaggery from somewhere nearby. Father ran to get the jaggery and brought it back. I was just a child then, but after eating the jaggery and drinking water, it felt like new energy surged through my body. Then we all set off again. Walking out in the heat for the puja, Mother's wisdom, Father fetching jaggery, and then continuing with renewed energy – all this was quite enchanting.

When Narendra Modi became chief minister of Gujarat, the circumstances in Vadnagar changed dramatically. When Heeraben was struggling

Maa's Sense of Service and Home Remedies

with her family in Vadnagar, there was no hospital to treat common ailments. In such times, her home remedies were a lifeline for many. People often referred to her as 'Doctor Ba' because of her knowledge and healing touch.

Though Vadnagar now has access to government and private hospitals, it was Heeraben who had served as the community's first line of healthcare. Back then, if someone fell ill, they had to travel to Gandhinagar, more than seventy kilometres away, and there were no health schemes like Ayushman Bharat offering free treatment to the poor.[1] Heeraben's selflessness meant that she helped countless people, and her actions likely influenced Narendra Modi's policies. As chief minister of Gujarat, Modi created various schemes for women, children and the elderly, and after becoming prime minister, these initiatives were expanded across the country.

As health minister of India Mansukh Laxmanbhai Mandaviya informed Parliament in 2024, 'More than 10,000 Jan Aushadhi centres have saved people ₹7,416 crore this fiscal year, and in nine years, this scheme has seen a 150-fold increase.'

17.

Mother's Political Message

A mother's support means everything to a child, and Heeraben always stood by her son, lifting his spirits when he needed it most. Their first public appearance together was on 30 January 1992, when Narendra Modi concluded his Ekta Yatra. The next day, a grand civic reception was organised in Ahmedabad in honour of all the unity marchers.

The Ekta Yatra, led by Murli Manohar Joshi and initiated by a young Narendra Modi, was a defining moment in his life. This yatra, passing through fourteen states from Kanyakumari to Srinagar, was a bold symbol of unity and defiance, launched at a time when terrorism was rampant in Punjab and Kashmir. On 26 January 1992, the national flag waved proudly at Lal Chowk in Srinagar, signalling not just unity

Maa Heeraben and Narendra

but the resilience of India's history, values and national spirit. On this occasion, Heeraben was seen applying a tilak to her son.

As the philosopher Og Mandino says, there is no mantra for success. There is no specific formula for it. Narendra Modi's success was no different. It was the product of intense dedication and discipline, with Heeraben's sacrifices and prayers behind him every step of the way. Despite his rise to political prominence, Heeraben never sought any special treatment or privileges from her son. Even when he became chief minister of Gujarat and later prime minister of India, she never asked for anything. She visited Delhi only once at his insistence but soon returned to Gujarat, feeling her presence might disrupt his work.

Heeraben is like that light which enters a dark room through a small hole and illuminates the entire space. This reminds me of a saying by Kahlil Gibran: 'My home says to me, "Do not leave me, for here is your past," and my road says to me, "Come, follow me, for I am your future."' For Heeraben, her home was everything – a place here she could move around as she pleased in her three-room flat, read her Gita and sit on her chair for hours, saying her prayers. There were

Mother's Political Message

no servants or maids in her home. If she needed a little help, she would take assistance from Pankaj. She was content there; she found peace in her routine. Her mornings were dedicated to hymns and prayers, and in the evenings, people from the neighbourhood would come, and she would chat with them.

Heeraben was a woman of simplicity. Her home was her sanctuary. Despite her son's growing political stature, she remained out of the public eye, preferring solitude.

In 2001, when Narendra Modi became chief minister of Gujarat, he sought his mother's blessings. Heeraben, unaware of the full significance of his new role, simply wished him well and asked him never to accept bribes. Modi often recalled this moment, highlighting it as a foundational lesson in his life. In 2002, Heeraben's statement, 'My son loves everyone,' became famous when she recounted a story about Modi giving away a coin he had found to a poor girl for books. She knew her son's heart reflected his values – values she had instilled in him.

In 2014, on his sixty-fourth birthday, Heeraben surprised Modi by giving him a donation of ₹5,001 for the Jammu and Kashmir Flood Relief

Fund. It was a gesture that spoke volumes about her quiet but unwavering support. After the demonetisation of 2016, Heeraben stood in line at a bank in Gandhinagar like any ordinary citizen, showing her solidarity with her son's decision. Though the Opposition criticised Modi for making his mother stand in line, Heeraben remained unfazed. She didn't seek any special treatment, even as the mother of the prime minister.

Even at the age of ninety-nine, Heeraben was seen waiting in line at a polling booth, this time in a wheelchair. There was no security, no VIP treatment – just a mother casting her vote, not as the mother of the prime minister. When the world was gripped by the COVID-19 pandemic, Heeraben set an example by getting vaccinated, sending a powerful message about the importance of the vaccine.

Modi's connection with his mother was deeply personal. Their meetings were always in her simple home, where he would seek her blessings and enjoy her homemade food. There was no pomp, no ceremony – just the tender, unconditional love of a mother. On her hundredth birthday, Modi shared that his mother's advice to

Mother's Political Message

him was always simple: 'Work with wisdom, live life with purity.'

Throughout his remarkable rise, Modi never lost sight of his roots. When he reached the highest offices in the land, he remained the son who would touch his mother's feet, seek her blessings and cherish her love. Whether he was chief minister of Gujarat or prime minister of India, his respect for Heeraben remained unchanged. On every birthday, during election campaigns and after every electoral victory, he would visit her for her blessings, reaffirming the importance of her guidance in his life.

Today, as Narendra Modi continues to carve out his legacy on the world stage, it is clear that behind every step of his journey is the unshakeable foundation laid by his mother – her sacrifices, wisdom and love.

18

When Narendra Modi Speaks of His Mother

It is said that not only does God shape humans but devoted humans also shape God. A mother, in this sense, is truly divine. While Narendra Modi rarely spoke about his family in public, his mother was always present in his speeches – her wisdom, stories and examples were a constant source of inspiration. In times of crisis, his first thought was always, 'Mother!' Whenever he felt troubled, he would either visit her or call for her. At every stage of his life, his mother was by his side.

In *Premtirth*, a compilation of stories written during his youth, Narendra Modi writes, 'The pure stream of maternal love is flowing like the continuous Saraswati.' Modi learned from his mother that true education isn't about formal schooling but about values and wisdom. Her foresight and simplicity always amazed him. In speeches, Modi often points to his mother as an example of strength. In a speech given on 25 January 2004 at Yugandhara Pratishthan Rakt Shakti, Jamnagar, Modi said, 'If you want to experience the power of women, look at a scene. Who sits on the two most powerful creatures in the world – a tiger and a lion? This is not a small matter. We have never thought about it. It is the power of women that rides on a tiger and a lion. Women are the power punch.' He explained that in many cultures women are not seen as divine, but India is unique in revering goddesses like Durga, Saraswati and Amba.

Elaborating on the strength of women, he said, 'How should the strength of a woman be measured?' He gave the example of a woman who burns her fingers while making rotis. Immediately she applies ointment to her fingers while blowing on them, all the while waiting anxiously for her husband to come home so that she can derive some comfort from him. Later, when she goes to buy vegetables in the market and hears news of a fire in her neighbourhood, she rushes home to see her neighbours trying to quell the flames by throwing dirt or water on the fire. She rushes in, crying, 'Oh, my child is still inside!' Without wasting a moment, that woman jumps into the blazing fire to save her child. No one else dares to enter the burning house. But the woman doesn't give up until she brings her child to safety. Modi says, 'The mother who keeps blowing on her hands for fifteen minutes due to the steam from the roti is the real manifestation of strength. She is prepared to jump into a burning house to save her child. This is female power, and this is the true form of a mother.'[1]

Modi's deep emotional bond with his mother remains a key influence in his life. During a conversation with Facebook founder Mark Zuckerberg in the US, he became teary-eyed remembering his mother's worries and sacrifices, her dedication to the family and her concern for her son.

A mother's greatness is beyond measure – she is truly priceless.

19

Guru's Service Was Rendered, But...

Life is often compared to a journey full of obstacles – thorns, crevices and mountains – that shape our path. It is by dealing with these struggles that we find our strength. True satisfaction comes from overcoming challenges, as easy achievements lack meaning. While all humans desire immortality, it is through our actions that we can achieve it. As the poet Ramdhari Singh Dinkar writes in *Urvashi*, 'I am human, desires flow within me. Sometimes slowly, sometimes fiercely, I twist the roots of my deeds.' People often lose themselves in their desires, unable to discern which ones are worth pursuing. Just as a craftsperson shapes clay, life's circumstances shape our priorities. Though all must eventually leave this world, some immortalise themselves through their wisdom and deeds.

Maa Heeraben and Narendra

In his years of service with the Sangh, Narendra Modi demonstrated the same dedication as a traveller on a long journey. He showed an unparalleled commitment to serving his guru, a service that remains an ideal for many. When I was writing *The Real Modi*, I met several people involved in the Sangh's work who shared their experiences of Narendra Modi's devotion to his guru, Lakshmanrao Inamdar. Modi's mentor was a great soul who taught him valuable lessons about austerity, knowledge, work and struggle. A young Narendra began attending the local RSS branch in the evenings at a time when the RSS was growing rapidly as a disciplined force, and Narendra found joy in participating in intellectual debates and discussions. Lakshmanrao, also known as Vakil Sahab, was renowned for his honesty and legal acumen. He welcomed young Narendra as a 'child volunteer' and began teaching him the true meaning of selfless service.

In 1967, when Narendra Modi returned from his journey in the Himalayas, there was no place for family happiness, but Narendra stopped for a while and once again went to an RSS branch, where he could contact his mentor, Vakil Sahab.

Guru's Service Was Rendered, But...

Andy Marino writes that Vakil Sahab was ready to take him under his protection again, but this time 'as a man not a boy'. In the 1970s, Narendra once again sought out his guru. Through his actions, he impressed Vakil Sahab so much that the latter began to see him as his successor. This mentoring lasted for eighteen months, and in the end, Narendra was awarded the official position of a propagandist in the RSS. The bond between the guru and the disciple was unbreakable, which both upheld throughout their lives.

Here Vivekananda's words hold great significance: 'Greatness is not achieved in moments. Do not back down from small beginnings; great deeds come afterwards, so be brave. Instead of dominating others, try to serve them. Moving forward selfishly and uncontrolled in the flow of life sinks even good ships.'

Lakshmanrao Inamdar was tending a plant whose shade everyone would receive in the coming years. There is folklore that perfectly encapsulates the bond between the guru and the disciple. In the far southern part of India, a king disguised himself and roamed the city incognito to understand the true state of his kingdom. He believed that people took care to show their king only beautiful things. The king in disguise saw an old man every day who planted saplings – not seasonal plants with ordinary flowers but fruit-bearing and shade-giving trees that took years to grow and lived for centuries. The king was astonished. He thought, 'Why is this old man planting these fruit-bearing and shade-giving trees? He will neither be able to enjoy their shade nor eat their fruit.' One day the king went to the old man and said, 'I should not intervene, but I want to ask a question. You will never see these trees mature, so why are you working so hard?' The old man replied, 'I may not witness their beauty, nor enjoy their shade, nor taste their fruit, but these benefits will certainly be reaped by future generations. I am carrying forward the thoughts of my ancestors.'

These trees planted by Lakshmanrao Inamdar are like Narendra Modi. The guru and disciple complemented each other. It was not Lakshmanrao Inamdar who became immortal by consuming that shade and its fruits, but he surely became immortal as Narendra Modi's guru.

On 5 February 2024, I went to Pune to attend a programme by Govind Giriji Maharaj, and I asked him about the time he first came into

Guru's Service Was Rendered, But...

contact with Narendra Bhai. He told me that they met when Vakil Sahab was very ill. Narendra Modi had stayed in Pune to serve him.

In *Setubandh*, Narendra Modi writes, 'The period from 1981 to 1985 was the last phase of his life.' In that period of time Vakil Sahab lost his mother and younger brother, as well as his friends Keshavrao Deshmukh, Arvind Bhai Maniyar and Babu Bhai Ojha. 'One harsh blow after another was unbearable for Vakil Sahab. He was suffering from cancer, and his condition deteriorated day by day. As per his wish, Vakil Sahab was brought from the hospital to the Sangh office in Motibagh on 25 June 1985. He could only consume a few liquid items. But slowly, he became weaker, and the medication became ineffective. He couldn't speak either. During this time, sarsanghchalak Balasaheb came to meet him. Both were silent, but tears were flowing from their eyes. On the evening of the 14th, Vakil Sahab's condition worsened; his breathing and pulse slowed down. The time had come to complete his life's journey. At 2.30 a.m., his eyes closed. A saint departed from this world, but amidst all this, he left behind a radiant aura through which India is shining.'[1]

Narendra Modi was fortunate to serve his guru.

Pankaj Modi shared an incident related to Damodar Das Modi's last moments. 'Our father had bone marrow cancer. His health was deteriorating slowly. Narendra Bhai was on the Kailash Manasarovar Yatra at that time. There was only one word on Father's lips: "Kumar, call Kumar." Our father affectionately called Narendra Bhai Kumar. I had noted down the news of Father's illness at the Bharatiya Janata Party office so that whenever Narendra Bhai called the party, they could inform him. When Narendra Bhai returned from the Kailash Manasarovar Yatra, he brought holy water from there. As soon as Narendra Bhai poured the water into Father's mouth, within moments, Father left us all.'

Pankaj said emotionally, 'The entire family was stunned. It felt as if Father had waited only to meet Narendra Bhai.'

When I was writing *The Real Modi*, I met Sanjay Bhai Shah, who lives in Ahmedabad. He told me that his father, Rasik Bhai Magan Bhai Shah, and Narendra Bhai were very good friends. When Narendra Modi stayed at the Sangh office in Ahmedabad, he would visit Magan Bhai's

Guru's Service Was Rendered, But...

house at least once a week. Sanjay Bhai shared, 'At the time when my father's health deteriorated significantly, Narendra Bhai was on a trip to America. This must have been around 1992–1993. Narendra Bhai arranged for a complete report of my father's illness from America and consulted specialists there. An expert team of doctors was sent to our home.' Sadly, Narendra Modi, who is so devoted to serving others, was deprived of the opportunity to serve his own father.

In a letter Narendra Modi wrote about his father, 'As long as Father was alive, he took care not to burden anyone.' When his mother fell ill and was admitted to the hospital, Narendra Modi was deeply engrossed in his duties towards the nation. Narendra Modi says, 'With the motherland as our top priority, we must work together. The whole world is watching India. To maintain this trust, every Indian must devote all their strength. We must work every day, every moment for the nation's development. We cannot stop in our service to the nation.'

When Heeraben was admitted to the hospital due to certain health issues, she didn't have any serious health concerns. Narendra Modi wrote in an article about his mother, 'My mother never

Maa Heeraben and Narendra

wanted to be a burden on anyone. She always said, "I don't want anyone to serve me when I'm dying, I just want to quietly leave."' Heeraben did exactly that, she didn't take any help from any family member. When Heeraben was admitted to the hospital, Pankaj Modi, who usually stayed with her, was also away from Ahmedabad. Heeraben quietly departed. She didn't say anything to anyone or express any desires, she just left.

Narendra Modi cherished memories of his mother. Just a few days before, he had washed her feet, applied the water to his forehead like a tilak and sought her blessings. But in the end, Narendra, who dedicated himself every day to serving the motherland, couldn't be with his mother, much like a soldier who cannot be with his family in the joys and sorrows of serving Mother India.

Human life is short and filled with uncertain joys. Everyone, from kings to common people, faces death. True knowledge lies in recognising one's ignorance. Contentment is greater than wealth.

20

Heeraben's Cuisine: A Taste of Love and Nostalgia

Some of life's most joyful moments are when a mother lovingly feeds her child. Even as adults, many of us long to taste our mother's homemade cooking. Heeraben Modi learned the art of cooking at a young age. Her father, Hargovinddas Dajjidas Modi, ran a small eatery in Visnagar. It was in this humble environment that Heeraben developed her culinary skills, guided by her parents. In times of adversity, true talents often emerge.

According to the Narendra Modi app, Heeraben prepared a variety of dishes for her family. Despite their modest means, she made the most of what was available, infusing each meal with love and care. After her marriage to Damodar Das Modi,

Maa Heeraben and Narendra

Heeraben and her favourite child enjoying a meal prepared by her

Heeraben continued to cook for her family in Vadnagar. Damodar Das's tea business required a daily supply of milk, so Heeraben would make curd, butter and ghee herself.

Narendra Modi's childhood friend Ishwar Patel fondly remembers Heeraben's crisp pakoras, a dish that became a favourite among those who had the privilege of tasting her cooking. Modi's sister, Basanti, recalls the special dishes Heeraben would prepare during festivals, including shira – a sweet, aromatic dessert – and puris, which were always made with extra care. Basanti also highlighted Narendra's deep fondness for khichdi, a simple yet comforting dish that his mother prepared in various ways, catering to his tastes. Abbas,

Heeraben's Cuisine

Modi's Muslim friend and classmate, also shared his memories of Heeraben's generosity, particularly during festivals, when she would make him special meals like sweet sevaiya. Abbas recalled a particularly touching moment when, before he left for the Hajj pilgrimage, Heeraben not only gave him homemade snacks for the journey but also sent him money to help with his travel. These personal anecdotes paint a vivid picture of Heeraben's warmth and her role in creating a loving, inclusive atmosphere in the family, where food was not just sustenance but a way to express care, kindness and respect for others.

Heeraben always encouraged her children to learn and connect with nature, allowing Narendra Modi to swim for hours in the pond and teaching him to care for cows from childhood. Despite their family's financial struggles, they never compromised their dignity, and of Maa Heeraben's contributions to shaping her children's lives remain unforgettable.

Her greatest test came when she allowed Narendra to pursue his ascetic path, yet she sent him off with grace, embodying a mother's sacrifice and dedication. Maa Heeraben's influence went beyond mere sustenance; she instilled a deeper sense of purpose and values in her family.

While the Modi family had no political connections, from an early age, Narendra showed an eagerness to serve others. Whether it was organising funds to repair a school wall, serving tea to soldiers on trains or his keen interest in national issues, his actions were remarkable for someone so young. The seeds of these values were planted by his mother, whose teachings continue to guide him.

As Modi ventured further into politics, his mother's lessons on truth, sacrifice and service remained a constant source of strength and guidance. Whenever he faced political challenges, it was her wisdom that gave him the courage to persist.

Every mother in this country teaches her child to love God, stay away from sin and show empathy towards those in distress. One must have a pure heart to see God. Wisdom doesn't require scholarship; it requires a heart like that of a child. When a person reaches their goal, the soul illuminates, brightening life. Moral character and great strength emerge within a person, making life truly meaningful.

Heeraben's Cuisine

Heeraben is no longer in this world, but her life reflected similar ideals. She learned something from every event in her life. Her mother's passing soon after her birth, taking responsibility for so many siblings at a young age, missing school – none of these would have been easy. The absence of a mother in childhood is a painful regret for anyone because a mother is the one who teaches the good and bad in life, teaches you what to do and what not to do. What must have gone through Heeraben's mind during that time? How many dreams must have passed through that childlike mind, but surrounded by responsibilities, did she have to leave all these behind? After marrying Damodar Das Modi and arriving in Vadnagar, a new world opened up for her. Both husband and wife worked hard together to steer the household forward. Heeraben did not have a formal education, but she knew the values and goals of life. It is said, 'Everyday difficulties shape the words of life.'

Today, Heeraben Modi stands as an inspiration to millions of mothers, not just in India but around the world.

Notes

Chapter 1 Maa Is Gone

1 In an interview aired on Aaj Tak, 20 December 2022.
2 https://www.narendramodi.in/mother.

Chapter 2 Maa's Childhood and Challenges

1 Sanjay Pokhriyal, 'From the Pages of History: When the Flag of Freedom Revolution Was Hoisted in Nagpur on 18 June 1923', *Jagran*, 12 June 2022, https://www.jagran.com/lifestyle/miscellaneous-when-the-flag-of-freedom-revolution-was-hoisted-in-nagpur-jagran-special-22796403.html#.

Chapter 3 Family Responsibility

1 https://www.narendramodi.in/mother.

Notes

Chapter 4 Mother the Teacher, Narendra the Disciple

1. See Kishor Makwana's *Samajik Samrasta*, a collection of Narendra Modi's public speeches.

Chapter 6 From Birth to School: Mother's Influence on Narendra Modi

1. A.P.J. Abdul Kalam and Arun Tiwari, *Wings of Fire* (Universities Press, 1999).

Chapter 8 Father's Teachings

1. 'PM Modi in Aligarh: Aligarh's Muslim Locks Were My Father's Friends ... PM Modi Narrated the Story', Aaj Tak, 14 September 2021.
2. Arvind Chaturvedi, *The Real Modi* (Bloomsbury, 2020), 35.

Chapter 9 Heeraben's Concerns

1. Chaturvedi, *The Real Modi*, 78–79.
2. Andy Marino, *Narendra Modi: A Political Biography* (HarperCollins Publishers, 2014), 34.

Notes

Chapter 10 Family Livelihood and Parental Imparting: A Boon for Politics

1. 'PM Narendra Modi in Conversation with Actor Akshay Kumar', posted on 24 April 2019 by Narendra Modi, YouTube.
2. Marino, *Narendra Modi*, 29.
3. Narendra Modi, *Social Harmony*, ed. Kishore Makwana (Prabhat Prakashan, 2015), 195.

Chapter 13 Blessings and Counsel

1. Marino, *Narendra Modi*.

Chapter 15 Narendra's Asceticism, Mother's Support

1. Narendra Modi, 'It is my fortune to witness the consecration of Ram Lalla in Ayodhya', X, 11 January 2024.

Chapter 16 Maa's Sense of Service and Home Remedies

1. The Ayushman Bharat Pradhan Mantri Jan Arogya Yojana (AB-PMJAY) is a scheme implemented by

the National Health Authority. Its aim is to provide health cover of ₹5 lakh per family per year for 12 crore beneficiary families for admissions to secondary and tertiary care hospitals.

CHAPTER 18 WHEN NARENDRA MODI SPEAKS OF HIS MOTHER

1 Modi, *Social Harmony*, 195.

CHAPTER 19 GURU'S SERVICE WAS RENDERED, BUT...

1 Narendra Modi, *Setubandh* (Prabhat Prakashan, 2017).

About the Author

Arvind Chaturvedi is a senior journalist who was born in the abode of Maa Vindhyachal and spent most of his early years in the streets of Baba Vishwanath's city, Kashi. After earning a master's degree in sociology from Banaras Hindu University, he moved to Delhi to pursue a career in journalism.

His first book, *The Real Modi*, was published by Bloomsbury in Hindi and later in English and Gujarati, earning him accolades and fame. *Modi Ka Banaras* was his second book on Prime Minister Narendra Modi. This is his third book.